I0101877

Loving America to Death

2016 – Election Year

by N.L. Brisson

These essays were first posted at

The Armchair Observer

Loving America to Death 2016
Table of Contents

Introduction to 2016

January
1   -   To US
5   -   Our Flawed Immigration System, Our Bad
10   -   The GOP's Experiments In Social Services
14   -   Dumbledore/Obama Speaks At
Hogwarts/Congress
21   -   Our Cities/Metro Areas Need Attention
24   -   To The Other Pod People
28   -   Why I Pick Hillary In 2016

February
7   -   Regulating Wall Street
9   -   "You Say You Want A Revolution"
18   -   A Worried Democrat Ponders
25   -   Why We Can't Elect Donald Trump (Or
Any Of The Bully Boys)
28   -   Stopping Donald Trump

March
2   -   The GOP War On Women And Hillary
Clinton
13   -   Will We Duke It Out In The Streets
17   -   Trump Demographics

20 - Money And Hillary Clinton

24 - Who's To Blame?

April

1 - If You Are Not In The Game, Get Out Of The Way

10 - Who Will End Obstructionism?

12 - Global Concerns

19 - Sad That We Can't Discuss Politics

26 - I Blame Donald Trump

28 - Donald Trump's Way-Back Foreign Policy Machine

May

1 - Desert Dwellers And Polar Ice Caps

June

5 - Bernie Flaws

12 - Celebrating Hillary And History

14 - Implications Of Orlando And Beyond

24 - 2016 Elections: Should One Party Control All Three Branches Of Government?

28 - The Benghazi Report

July

6 - Shooting Black Folks Must Stop

18 - Donald Trump Is Deranged

21 - Donald Trump Is Deranged: The Details

24   -   The Last Great Conspiracy Theory?

August
24   -   The Republican Scandal Extravaganza
27   -   "In The Day" And Now/Black Power
29   -   The Bully v. The Work: The Presidential Debates
30   -   The Red Line - Syria Then And Now

September
9   -   Time For Single Payer Health Care
13   -   The Deplorables, The Republicans, And The Media

October
15   -   Hillary Clinton, Up Against Misogyny Is A Fight Girl
16   -   Sharknado Live, Death Throes Of The Dominant Male
18   -   Social Class And Hillary
22   -   Running Out Of Time
31   -   Hillary Emails: The Motherlode

November
14   -   Erasing The Sixties
17   -   Donald Trump And The Republications

December

3   -   What The Democratic Party Should Do,
Part 2
6   -   This Is The Dark Side
14   -   I Feel A Great Disturbance In The Force
19   -   Unfettered Capitalism Wins

January

To Us January 1, 2016

We live in the midst of a confusion of change and upheaval in these early years of the 21st century. Well the century is a 'teenager' so that might help explain some of the transitional chaos that we see around us. Some think that we are in the end times, and if they are Evangelicals they seem to believe that we can make these times even more difficult than they seem to be, or other think we can try to ease the planet into a functioning global unit without necessarily giving up our national identities. But we see social and actual earthquakes, cyclones, hurricanes, and floods going off like New Years Eve fireworks all round us.

Globally we have all of the death, migration, and destruction resulting from a Muslim world that is waking up to a realization that it must beat us or join us. We have coexisted peacefully with Muslim countries for a long time, although clashes have always occurred as far back as the days when the Middle East was the Western world's anvil of religious revelation.

We wonder if one religion might rule the world or if things will calm down among devout Fundamentalists and we will once again go back to a quieter tolerance of our differences. We wonder what we will do in nations that are at odds with Muslim Fundamentalism (I am opting for linguistic clarity over political correctness.) if we come face to face with their armies and their seeming anachronistic rules start to be forced upon us.

We wonder if the end result will be that the Middle East will reconsider its political and economic structures and share with its people some of the material comforts enjoyed in the rest of the world. We wonder if, as we move away from fossil fuels, these nations that are so dependent on them will find new resources to fuel their economies. Unless we can wrest some of the wealth away from those in the top 1% and make sure that people around the globe have ways to earn a living share of that wealth, I'm not sure we will be able to solve the ways that economic differences could continue to contribute to social chaos.

China has always been a secretive place, but not a very imperialistic place. They already own huge swaths of the globe and until recently that has been enough. But now that China is having its own rather late version of the Industrial Revolution and the Chinese people, who have not always had an abundance of even such essential commodities as food, see their standard of living rising or at least see that there will be opportunities to make their lives more comfortable, China's leaders must keep feeding these appetites or they may have an internal revolution on their hands. Besides China's leaders may be starting to think they might enjoy being a powerful force in the world. How will the rest of the nations, that have practiced imperialism and colonialism for centuries, convince China to stay away from military strength and land grabbing?

How will we deal with Putin, Syria, Assad, and Iran if they decide to become more and more militant? How will we spread the earth's resources, both natural and those made by man, to wipe out poverty? How will we insure that education is available to all people around the globe? We are far, far away from some of these goals. How will we continue to thrive if we have to cut back on the sources of power we now use to make the wheels of industry run? Can we take global warming and climate change into account even as we try to provide a good life for everyone on our planet? If we wean ourselves away from the fossil fuels we have come to depend on will we find enough resources to still live comfortably on a small planet with more and more people? Will we stay civilized or will we fall into an age of barbarity and struggle to survive? Will we ever be able to work together well enough to create a globe that is functional, or will we fail?

I do not see much cooperation as I look around me. I see people pulling mightily to hang on to things we will most likely have to let go of. I see people looking for their main chance as Europe and America seems to be facing more struggles. Changing times do give those, ruled by ambition and dreams of personal glory, chances to shuffle the power seats and declare themselves a, or even the world leader. Is the power in the world about to shift? How will that disadvantage us here in America? How will it disadvantage you in your corner of the world?

There is a lot going on right now and it is no great wonder that we feel nervous, anxious, or afraid. But we should also feel quite excited to be living in such a pivotal age. Yes, we could win all, or lose all, or end up in some kind of lengthy cultural limbo. But we are smart, we are creative, we are innovative, and we all want basically the same things. We want to be sure we can take care of our basic needs and those of our loved ones. We would love some peace of mind. And we would love to find our way through chaos to a new global economy that sustains us all.

We would like to go into space and find new frontiers to inhabit with our squabbles and our talents, our hatefulness and our beauty. Spreading out won't solve all mankind's problems as we will still contain both good and evil within us, but it will be engrossing, and it will keep us from feeling that we are coming to the end of something. I think if we all turn our eyes away from recreating what is past and toward designing a future we can all feel good about; then we can win another round for man and woman kind. It's a New Year and hope should always begin a New Year. To us!

Our Flawed Immigration System, Our Bad January 5, 2016

I hear America making many of the following points about immigrants, most of them are false because they are sweeping generalizations. They say, "immigrants take our jobs." "The government is using our tax dollars to provide benefits for undocumented immigrants." "Illegal immigrants vote fraudulently, and they usually vote for Democrats." "Undocumented workers will work for very low wages, and they therefore drive down wages of American workers" "White people would not be outnumbered by minorities if illegal immigrants were sent home." "We put illegal immigrants who break the law into American jails at taxpayer's expense." "Undocumented people have large families, and all of their children are born at no cost in American hospitals and automatically become citizens." "All illegal immigrants are from South of the Border."

"Undocumented and legal immigrants exclude us by refusing to learn our language." "When we see women in scarves or even long garments like burqas or hijabs, we think in our heart of hearts that this is not an American form of dress. We want women to take off these garments, which to us seem like symbols of female submission/oppression, to enjoy American fashions. We are afraid that people with such strong beliefs will impose their beliefs on us. They will bring Sharia law. We will find America becoming a Muslim nation."

I could go on and on. These are all things I have heard people say or have read in the media about immigrants, especially immigrants without legal documents. However, if we are perfectly honest it is America's shoddy system that allows people to come into our country and live and work with no documents, or stolen documents, or illegally obtained documents. Last week official admitted that we have not system for tracking people who stay after their visa has expired.

I read an interesting and prize-winning book called **Americanah** a few years ago by Chimamanda Ngozi Adichie, a Nigerian woman who came to America and had to stay until she could earn enough money to return home. She describes what she had to do to work in America without proper documents to earn tickets back to her home.

Some of the things we think are true of immigrants, both legal and illegal, have been researched and have been found to be false, or mostly false. But statistics do suggest that America will not be a majority white nation for much longer, or white people may have already slipped into the minority. Caucasians do not seem to be the wave of the future, and it may be too late to reproduce our way back into ascendancy. Deep down we feel good old American guilt over all these unfriendly or even hateful feelings. We are supposed to be the great melting pot where everyone shares the American Dream, deposits a few new wrinkles that make for a tasty cultural stew, and then puts nose to grindstone to climb the ladder of success.

We have dealt with groups that don't see owning things and amassing wealth and fitting in as important goals. But these groups have been small and scattered and have not had an enormous effect on the America work ethic or our materialism. Recent groups do not seem as interested in assimilating (although assimilation can take generations). To us it seems as if they cling to the language and culture of their nation of origin. This was true of previous groups also, such as the Irish and the Italians. I think that this time people are worried that America is not strong enough to shake off these new influences and maintain its European/Caucasian flavor. Will our grandchildren speak Spanish? Will they bow to Mecca? Some of these things we can't know.

Welcoming people and treating them well is more likely to keep America as is, than treating people with isolation and hostility. But it seems counter-intuitive to many to accept strangers, and it just seems plain wrong to accept people who came without going through the proper routes, and who do not possess the proper papers. (Although we don't rely much on fancy identity papers in America.) I don't know if these new immigrants will take over America (given that the Dream has gotten a bit thin for all of us) or if they will blend into and enhance American culture, and the only way to find out is to wait and see what happens.

But what I do wonder is how can we deport people who simply took advantage of a very lackadaisical visa system, or borders that are not secured (and my guess is they cannot be secured with violating the rights of citizens). We should leave immigrants who worked the loopholes (a very American thing to do) alone, grandfather them in, give them papers now, or after ten years, or whatever punishing delay, and then create a system that works. That probably will involve doing some very un-American things like using an electronic tracking system, or eyeball-ID or facial recognition at points of entry and exit.

We are a nation of people who love to look for loopholes and then use them to our advantage. These are obviously people after our own hearts. So, make sure that in the future we close the loopholes (not with walls) and recognize that whatever system we create in this age of jets will most likely not be perfect. Perhaps we will all have to put up with some kind of chemical or electrical ID markers in the not-so-distant future. However, this has one big problem – the greater the control, the less our privacy.

Our leaky immigration system is our bad; it is on us. How can we blame those who use our mistakes to seek material gains or to find a better life for their children? Isn't that what all our progenitors did?

The GOP's Experiments in Social Science
January 10, 2016

Take everyone off food stamps. These are the kinds of things a GOP candidate must say nowadays to get elected. Close the Housing Assistance Program and the program to which needy families can apply for emergency cash. This is Jeb Bush's newest election offer to the American people. Will it help him rise in the polls? Who cares? These are terrible ideas.

Let's set up a great big experiment with poor people. Let's deprive them of a means to an adequate diet and to adequate shelter. Oh, and let's deprive the disabled also, and old people. Let's see if being hungry and living in squalor will give them a new lease on life because it works so well in nations with no social services. Not.

Didn't I just spend two holiday weekends being bombarded with the same commercial with the sad, uplifting music begging me to send money each month to support starving children around the world? Happy Holidays! Any idea how it feels to pay for a supposedly free, possibly cheerful holiday movie with guilt because your income will not stretch far enough to help these children?

How will we feel when this is right outside our door (it already is), or when it's us? Many people in America still don't have jobs. You may believe that they could work if they wanted to but what if that is, for the most part, a big fat lie? What if there are not enough jobs for everyone, or what if the people do not have the skills to fit the jobs that are available? What if there are people who are untrainable for mental, or emotional, or physical reasons?

We have experimented with people before, but never on this large a scale, except perhaps the polio vaccine tests. It was inhuman when the Nazi's did it, and it is still not a humane way to behave. I know Bush says he will replace these social safety net programs with state grants so that states can fund their own programs. This is part of the Federalist mantra of the GOP – let's go back to 1783 and choose the strictest interpretation of state's rights that our forefathers considered and discarded. Let's take the other path and see where that one goes. In fact, Greg Abbott, the new governor of Texas is calling for a Constitutional Convention to rewrite the Constitution, and to beef up state's rights, among other things.

The Feds keep making people do things they don't want to do, Republicans whine. Southern states and others scattered throughout the US don't want a social safety net. They don't want illegal immigration. They don't want legal same-sex marriage, they want to teach creationism in their schools, they want to privatize schools, and on and on with these backward ideas. They want to use fossil fuels without limitations. They want to 'drill-baby-drill' until the whole of our beautiful land is devastated and toxic. They want our corporations back, and will sell out American workers by busting unions, and refusing to set a minimum wage, and using any ploy necessary to bring the Industrial Age back to America.

I don't think that any of it will work. It will just serve to dismantle our nation. You can't turn back the clock. The tolerance levels in the world have moved beyond their reactionary minds. If people lose their rights and their needs are not met they will fight to get it all back or the nation will see poverty like it has not seen in over a century. If you give money to the states, some states will just use it for another purpose. There are states that would not accept the ACA federal exchanges; the rich exercising their principles at the expense of the poor.

Better wake up now. You will not gain autonomy – you will lose economic security. I'm not saying that we could not benefit from a reevaluation of our social programs, or by tweaking them for greater effectiveness. But I'm saying that adopting a quick fix like turning the whole thing over to the states is not the answer. The inequalities between states will be quite stark if we follow this Federalist path.

I'm sure that when you have a job you will shut out the dire need around you, but when you don't there will be nothing to keep you from having to wallow in the mire with all the dispossessed. Wake up! This is not the South rising again. The Civil War was an awful war. If the nation does break up again I hope it does it quietly. Of course, I hope it doesn't happen at all. I did not think we would still be talking about this in 2016. Why do Americans seem to like these ideas? Do they not see the turmoil in the world? Do they not realize that they could be the one laid low? They are much closer to the bottom than the leaders they are following, who are not likely to ever end up poor.

These rich politicians made sure the fix was in. People will vote to have stuff taken away? Who knew?

Those wily Republicans say they cannot legislate to lessen climate change and global warming because they are not scientists. And yet they will swear they know how healing it will be to Americans if we take away the safety net even though they are neither economists nor social scientists. This suggest expertise is simply a matter of expediency. When leaders haul out reasoning that makes our brains feel like pretzels that is when we need to disregard them, instead of making the very stupid move of electing them. Aren't we tired of fighting these battles created by these very selfish people?

Dumbledore/Obama Speaks at Hogwarts/Congress January 14, 2016

I have defended Obama many, many times over the past 7 years, although he most likely knows nothing about it and he really didn't require my assistance. As I became more aware of the Republican agenda for America, I became more and more grateful that Obama was in the White House helping Democrats at least hold the line against the GOP extremists. While the right wing bemoaned the Stimulus, which was not an action that Obama did on his own, I was glad that we were not going to be held to an austerity that would have prolonged the Great Recession. While the right wing lashed out when Obama did an end run around them to pass the Affordable Care Act, I was glad that more people would have health insurance, that people with preexisting conditions would be covered, and that certain young family members would no longer have to rely on the emergency room for medical treatment.

I can see that America is not as prosperous as it was, at least not for all of us. I have not forgotten the parade of factories that have left empty buildings all over my hometown and the number of workers who once had secure, good paying jobs who now have jobs that pay much less. My town has not recovered from the recession, but they are working, and the job market has ticked up quite a bit from the days when there were no jobs to be found. I know the Obama years have helped our economy. The strides made with alternative energies alone will serve our economy and our environment well into the future.

Republicans have been aching to cut the social safety net, privatize social security, end Medicare and privatize schools. These things are bad policy, and Obama has held off these Social Darwinists for two terms now, two terms while Republicans complained bitterly and lied to the people and said that benefits are harmful. Obama has shepherded us through an era when facing up to our lingering racism has been painful and obvious, although still unresolved.

Watching the heart-wrenching confrontations
between the police and young black folks, with the
seemingly tiny or nonexistent misdemeanors being
met by out-of-all-proportion consequences, will force
us, I hope, to solve our divisions. Obama kept us
calm and called for solutions. I don't know how all of
this would have played out if we did not have Obama
in the White House.

Republicans vowed to block President Obama, and
they have done so throughout the Obama years, so
much so that I often wished for a referee who would
call foul and put a stop to all of the obstruction and
vituperation. Obama still steadily found ways to hold
back their extreme agenda and get things done. So,
they stonewalled in Washington, voted to repeal the
ACA eighty-five million times, voted to defund
Planned Parenthood, found ways to abuse traditional
perks like gerrymandering to pack statehouses with
Republicans and ways to set voting rights back 50
years, ways to keep Obama from appointing liberals
in the courts, and still Obama did what he could for
Americans day after day.

So, I loved President Obama's last SOTU address. I
felt like he was Dumbledore summing things us, the
good and the bad for all the students of Hogwarts
whether allies or enemies. I agree that we are still a
strong nation. I agree that civility is not dead,
although it sometimes seems that way. I believe that
we have done great things in the past, in the present,

and that in the future we will find a way to a new
prosperity. I believe we need to work together,
although I have little faith that the GOP fever has run
its course. They have waited almost eight years for
this moment, and even if it is not turning out quite as
planned, they can taste victory. But I will miss
Obama, and I will not take a GOP win as any kind of
victory because we will have to do things that we will
later have to undo, and because that will be a real
waste of time for America, and because it may actually
make our nation more vulnerable to those who hope
we fail. What we must do now is elect a Democrat
and, truth to tell, either Hillary or Bernie will do.
Better to have two good choices than fifteen bad
ones.

Our Cities/Metro Areas Need Attention
January 21, 2016

I live in a small city in the center of New York State
which has been hit hard by globalization. I know
some people blame trade agreements, or Obama, or
high taxes, but I do not. I think our corporations were
set to salivating at the thought of distant places with
very cheap labor, and no environmental regulations,
and low overhead. Once the first little lemming
jumped continents there was a stampede to the
newest Capitalist nirvana (a Communist country –
who would have thought). There was the added
incentive of all those brand-new consumers to satisfy.

Manufacturers saw an opportunity-vacuum and they filled it, because we know how nature abhors a vacuum. My small city lost business after business. Empty factories still sit everywhere or have been torn down or repurposed. Corporate names have disappeared from local landmarks. But what I was not seeing, or at least not clearly was brought to my attention by an online article. It was a study at the Century Foundation saying that my hometown, Syracuse, NY, had the most stubborn and segregated area of poverty in all of America. (https://apps.tcf.org/architeture-of-segregation)

Here are some excerpts from the article:

The Architecture of Segregation: Civil Unrest, the Concentration of Poverty and Public Policy by Paul A Gargowsky

"Over the past year, scenes of civil unrest have played out in the deteriorating inner-ring suburbs of Ferguson and the traditional urban ghetto of inner city Baltimore. The proximate cause of those conflicts has been brutal interactions between police and unarmed black men, leading to protests that include violent confrontations with police, but no single incident can explain the full extent of the protestor's rage and frustration. The riots and protests – which have occurred in racially-segregated, high-poverty neighborhoods, bringing back images of the "long, hot summers" of the 1960's – have sparked a national conversation about race, violence, and policing that is long overdue.

Something important, however, is being left out of this conversation: namely, that we are witnessing a nationwide return of concentrated poverty that is racial in nature, and that this expansion and continued existence of high-poverty ghettos and barrios is no accident. These neighborhoods are not the value-free outcome of the impartial working of the housing market. Rather in large measure, they are the inevitable and predictable consequences of deliberate policy choices."

"To address the root causes of urban violence, police community tensions, and the enduring legacy of racism, the genesis of urban slums and the forces that sustain them must be understood. As a first step in that direction, this report examines the trends in the population and characteristics of neighborhoods of extreme deprivation. Some of the key findings include:

- There was a dramatic increase in the number of high-poverty neighborhoods.
- The number of people living in high-poverty ghettos, barrios, and slums has nearly doubled since 2000, rising from 7.2 million to 13.8 million.

- These increases were well under way before the Great Recession began.

- Poverty became more concentrated – more than one in four of the black poor and nearly one in six of the Hispanic poor lives in a neighborhood of extreme poverty, compared to one in thirteen of the white poor.

- To make matters worse, poor children are more likely to reside in high-poverty neighborhoods than poor adults.

- The fastest growth in black concentration of poverty (12.6 percentage points) since 2000 was not in the largest cities, but in metropolitan areas with 500,000 to 1 million persons."

More from the study:

Public Policy and the Concentration of Poverty

Recent economic troubles have clearly contributed to the sharp re-concentration of poverty since 2000. But another huge factor, in good economic times and bad, has been rampant suburban and exurban development. Suburbs have grown so fast that their growth was cannibalistic: it came at the expense of the center city and older suburbs. In virtually all metropolitan areas, suburban rings grew much faster than was needed to accommodate metropolitan growth, so that the central cities and inner-ring suburbs saw massive population growth, so that the central cities and inner-ring suburbs saw massive populations declines. The recent trend toward gentrification is barely a ripple compared to the massive surge to the suburbs since about 1970. Moreover, taxpayers funded all the new infrastructure needed to facilitate suburban expansion – roads, schools, water and sewer, and so on – even as existing infrastructure was abandoned and underutilized in the urban core.

The population movements were also highly selective. Through exclusionary zoning and outright housing market discrimination, the upper-middle class and affluent could move to the suburbs, and the poor were left behind. Public and assisted housing units were often constructed in ways that reinforced existing spatial disparities. Now with gentrification driving up property values, rents, and taxes in many urban cores, some of the poor are moving out of central cities into decaying inner-ring suburbs."

Me again:

If you are like me, you have a few ideas about how to solve the decay in and around our cities. Jobs and a healthy economy would surely go a long way towards alleviating this downward trend, but recession alone does not explain why our minorities are so consistently poor and why they are so trapped in inner city neighborhoods where services are poor, budgets are tight, and people are not thriving.

If architecture and real estate have been used to discriminate then perhaps some attention to these areas may help get us out of this stubborn pattern. Even if we don't find ways to get our economy humming along again, we still need to tackle this stuff. With smaller local budgets at all levels (think Flint, Michigan) we will need to be really creative, really compassionate, and practice lots of tolerance and civility that we believe in so strongly but which we are having such a hard time accessing. Solving housing problems might also help solve the problems in some of our schools. And it might free up the creativity of people who are too busy surviving to tap into their higher order skills.

To the Other Pod People January 24, 2016

I have a few things to say to the disenchanted voters, the disillusioned, the world-weary, the cynical, the dropouts, the cop outs, and all Americans who say that they believe our government is so corrupt and our politicians are such crooks that they cannot stir themselves to cast a vote in any election. These folks (and I have heard mostly men speak like this, although I am sure that there are women who feel this way also) think that not voting makes a statement, that opting out of the system will eventually crash the system. Some want to reboot to a better, fairer government, some want anarchy, a government which exercises no control at all. Oh yes, let's put 7+ billion people on a small planet and see what happens when the rules are 'every man for himself,' and when there is no centralized fund to spend on, well, anything. Whose idea of nirvana is that?

If these people who choose not to vote stick us with a government run by a Tea Party extremist, I hope they are the first among us to realize what a mistake it was not to vote. People who don't vote are actually voting for someone, but they get to do it passively and they get no blame if the next 'power people' do not best represent the needs of the nation. Circumstances matter in an election. Democracy requires participation. People all over the world are disenfranchised and have no right to vote or their vote is just for show. We could live in a nation like Syria with a leader like Assad who does not mind turning over half of the citizens into refugees to burden other nations. The Syrians had to vote with their feet, sometimes their lives, and they had to leave their possessions behind. We could live in a nation lie North Korea which apparently starves its citizens to build a hydrogen bomb that will threaten America.

When you opt out of voting you are making choices for all of us. You are cynical, you are arrogant. You think you are an arbiter of truth and a punisher of failure or unfairness, but you help bad government thrive. There are no perfect people; there are no perfect governments. Perhaps your vote does not carry the weight it once did. Not voting will not cure this. Those who sin are thrilled that you didn't vote. They counted on it. Those who lost cannot be helped by you in any way, even if those losers would have been best for our nation's future. You have not been sidelined. You have sidelined yourselves. How will our nation ever improve its ways if people who are intelligent enough to be disillusioned are spineless enough to go to their corner and pout about it? You folks who have disenfranchised yourselves are getting on my last nerve. You are the other pod people. Please take a stand for something and vote.

Why I Pick Hillary in 2016
January 28, 2016

I am a girl. Hillary is a girl. I'm with Hillary. I would not back Hillary just because she is a girl, but she is also a girl who has an agenda for America that is well thought-out and based on plenty of experience. In addition, I assume that she will be flexible enough to adopt a new approach to a problem if she is convinced that it will be more effective. And I feel certain that she will not turn into a Republican anytime soon. I love Bernie Sanders, I do. His people make an ad for him with Simon and Garfunkel's

"America" song from the Bookends Album. It warms my hippie soul. If I didn't think it was time for a girl President, then that little revolutionary in me would go for Bernie. But right now, the only way I will pick Bernie is (1) if he turns into a girl (highly unlikely), or (2) if he wins the Democratic nomination.

Girls, ladies, women, females have always been asked to wait. Wait for this, wait for that, and when we felt it was appropriate, which we usually did because we are pragmatic and compassionate, we did wait. I don't think we have to wait in 2016. I think we are good to go. So, I back Hillary Clinton and all the other women who have worked so hard in the past eight years to keep the rights that women have won – rights that never came easily. So, I also stand with Cecile Richards and Planned Parenthood, and I stand with Emily's List trying to get more women elected to office, and a whole roster of active women that I won't list because then I'll forget someone and I'll feel badly about it.

I sure would like to hear Hillary Clinton addressed as Madame President and I know those other women will be there to help the first woman President in America do a truly great job. Now that will be huge! (Okay, I was wrong about this. But not about everything.)

February

Regulating Wall Street February 7, 2016

Can we afford to mess with Wall Street? Isn't it the tick tock heartbeat that keeps our Capitalist economies alive? I picture an endless cycle of regulatory action and Wall Street vengeance. The whole idea of an index of economic health that is built around putting down a bet on whether a company or commodity will turn a profit strikes me as a ridiculously unstable structure on which to base an economy, or my retirement income. However, that is the system we have. As the Industrial Age moves on to distant corners (from us) of the globe the Stock Market has experienced ever more volatility and is less and less under our control. American companies do not have factories in America, they don't pay taxes in America, but they still hold places on the American Stock Exchange (and other Stock Exchanges). And, although for many years our Stock Market pretty much set the pace around the world that is no longer as true. There are Stock Markets in a number of countries that can send shock waves through ours.

The "creative" way that the stock brokerage companies in America met the changes in the industrial scene in America should have been and probably were illegal. However even if they were not sure about whether or not what they were doing was illegal, they knew it was risky. Perhaps is was not illegal because no one ever actually thought of doing something as stupid as bundling up bad mortgages with good mortgages and rating the whole bundle according to the best mortgages in the bundle. What is clear is that someone at these stock brokerage firms knew that these bundles reeked and that there might/would be financial repercussion. This does not even touch the illegality of the banks and mortgage companies that offered these mortgages in the first place.

Our economy, obviously, can't take too much of this kind of "black hat" creativity. We watched in horror as banks foreclosed on house after house, forcing Americans to scramble for new living arrangements and sometimes creating whole neighborhoods of empty houses. The Stock Market took a nosedive. My pension (and those of many Americans) took a nosedive. Employment took that same dive. Without the TARP I don't think we would have pulled up before we hit rock bottom. Without the stimulus we may have already had the revolution we could still be headed for.

It stands to reason that the argument that we might have to regulate Wall Street, make some rules about what is legal to do and what it is not legal to do has gained traction. This is what many Americans like about Elizabeth Warren and Bernie Sanders. We are justifiably angry at greedy hedge fund operators and mortgage companies for almost destroying the American economy and we don't just want reform, we want punishment. Hillary Clinton has also said that some regulation is necessary, although she does not hook into people's anger and does not seem to want to tar and feather the perpetrators, and then run them out the finance business. Mostly, we would be happy if they had to give us back what we lost because of their adventures in edgy economics.

But as for the future, for me, and perhaps for you, there are questions. First, since no one could have foreseen the bundling and sale of those stinky mortgages can we ever foresee every new ploy these people, who must make money or die, can think up? Second, can the American Stock Market provide the investment structure, and the secure economic base America needs any more at all? How would America function without a Stock Market? Can we overregulate the Stock Market and crash it? How do we choose the exact regulations that will protect us from illegal profiteering and yet will allow the Stock Market enough room to keep ticking along? If the SEC is unable to oversee the market, can we whip it into shape without putting a straitjacket on it?

Although I hate what brokerage firms did to us to attempt to make money from bad mortgages, I go back to my very first question – can we afford to mess with Wall Street? And if so, how much? I think we are afraid, we are very afraid, because we are not sure about the fragility of our economy, and the entire global economy. I have a gut feeling we should buck up the economy before we decide about large scale regulation of the Stock Market, or even perhaps the "Big Banks." Despite our very real anger and our desire to send a tough message through punishment. I also have a gut feeling that effective oversight is important to stop truly risky financial strategies that could still be invented by both the Stock Market and the banks.

So, I am feeling that more information about exactly what regulation would look like and what the effects of any regulation, or various specific regulation measures, might be. This is a time when we need to look to our economists. We also need to remember that economics is hardly an exact science and that economists have differing points of view on these matters, which may be influenced by famous economists, or by their politics, or both. What we decide, even after input from the field, will still require a final judgment on the part of each of us. Please, all you economic geeks, use simple language that we can all understand and perhaps some scenarios like the ones they used in the film, **The Big Short**, to illustrate your points.

"You Say You Want a Revolution"
February 9, 2016

Revolution is in the air once again. When I was a younger person in the 60's we talked about revolution incessantly. We had so many good reasons for wanting change. We were losing our guys in a war that seemed to have nothing to do with us, in a faraway tropical place called Vietnam. We were watching our policemen, our National Guardsmen, and our elected officials turn fire hoses on peaceful black folks who just wanted to be granted the equality they were supposed to have won long before. Separate but equal was very obviously not equal at all (still isn't). Women had the "pill" and we were stunned by the implications of that.

We were often granted dispensation from harsh punishment while we indulged peacefully in the illegal practice of getting high in public. We probably were treated gently for a while because the people in local power were our parents, and they tried to let us express ourselves. Besides there were so many of us, all walking around in our flowery clothing imported from Mexico and India, and wearing flowers in our hair, and smiling in gentle understanding, even when practicing civil disobedience as demonstrated by Martin Luther King, et al. All the lovely people would gather at outdoor concerts with happy half-dressed children running everywhere and bubbles in the pungent air. We were the very revolution we sought, and we thought that our very existence would change America forever, and perhaps it did. However, the intensity of the movement subsided, despite our feeling that it would make America forever new and better. There have been many effects on US politics that can be traced back to the peaceful revolution of the 60's and the 70's. But the fervor we once felt for a new kind of authenticity got syphoned away by American materialism and we joined the race for the old American Dream of owning lovely things and creating cushy comfort for ourselves and our families. Not that we gave up all of our zeal for lifting up those who did not yet share our comfort, but it began to be subsumed under the old adage that 'charity begins at home.'

So now we are being aroused to a new revolution and, clearly, we need one. Our American Democracy has almost disappeared into the pockets of the wealthy few among us. It is clear to some of the 99.9% that there is too much money being flashed around, and too much of the influence it buys in our political system. We the people are being sidelined because we cannot compete with a system where influence is purchased. We have numbers but we are not using the force of our majority very effectively. It is assumed that folks without wealth will rise up and demand our government back from the wealthy, although I have not seen many signs that this is the way events will unfold. The Occupy movement is the closest that we have come to mass demonstrations and that did not last very long or have much of an effect on those in power. We are too complacent or stupefied or in some way apolitical to even use the power of the vote. We seem happy to troll from the sidelines, and we are not unified at all. We are the most divided we have been since, perhaps, the Civil War.

Bernie Sanders talks about revolution and some people swoon. I assume he means a peaceful revolution which will stay within the bounds of the Constitution and the present-day configuration of our government. But in these times of such a passionate partisan divide is a revolution a good idea? Will it go nuclear, or can it be kept away from mayhem? Would even a quiet revolution split America apart right now? Would the militias bring out the guns? Have Democrats been stockpiling guns? I don't think I could bear another Civil War, and I only experienced the first one at a considerable dusty remove. Could you watch America get torn apart? Would it come to that? "You say you want a revolution," but maybe these are not the times to be incendiary. Maybe we need some of that famous diplomacy so maligned by the Republicans that Obama has put his faith in. Perhaps I have done that terrible getting-more-conservative-as-I-get-older thing, or perhaps I am just chickening out. I do think there are many things that we need to change in order that we all thrive in the future, something which seems not in the least guaranteed as matters stand right now.

I don't want to see our nation "ripped asunder" and considering how divided we are at this time and how passionately people defend positions that are opposites, becoming two Americas seems more than a likely outcome of holding the revolution in 2016. I have revolution in my soul so I could perhaps be swayed by sound arguments in favor of such a movement. But mostly I think that the skill required to keep this revolution from getting out of hand seems beyond our normal style of throwing bills at problems and hoping they become laws that fix things.

A Worried Democrat Ponders
February 18, 2016

It all sounded so simple. The Dems would back Hillary Clinton, but they did not want her to run alone. They wanted a primary – a sort of pro forma affair, just to keep her on her toes. She was the anointed. In fact, it seemed as if they needed Hillary because she was experienced, but they didn't really "feel" Hillary. There was a last-minute groundswell for Elizabeth Warren. When Bernie Sanders entered the race, along with Martin O'Malley and Jim Webb, none of these male candidates seemed strong enough to change the course of the Democratic Party's push to elect the first female President of the United States. O'Malley and Webb were virtual unknowns, not hefty enough in personality, experience, or cultural cachet to be any real force in the primaries. Bernie Sanders was a Socialist for heaven's sakes. Americans shudder at the faintest whiff of "socialism."

The exigencies of the current state of our nation are perceived by shell-shocked Americans with great anxiety. Faced with an economy far less favorable than projected there is unexpected appeal in a senior citizen who, philosophically, has remained in the 1960's for decades, and who preaches a revolutionary message that has finally found its powerful rebirth. This has become a phenomenon that is changing everyone's predictions about who will be the Democratic candidate in 2016.

I have found such solidarity with fellow Democrats, all resolved that we must not let a Republican win the Presidency in 2016. That goal is even more important now with the Supreme Court suddenly in play. Bernie's success is splitting Democrats in the Hillary camp). Most Hillary people say they will support Bernie if he is the party's candidate. The reverse is not likely to be true, however. Some Bernie people say that they would rather vote for a Republican than for Hillary Clinton. How is that even a thing? The

Republican's agenda is in no way similar to that of the Democrats. Perhaps there is a strong desire to be a firebrand, an extremist – any extreme will do. It is as if there is no middle anymore.

It doesn't help that Bernie gets such sweet media attention. The media loves Bernie. The media also puts on a sour fact for anyone who is not an extremist. And Bernie has been nice. He has been the ever-well-received 'happy warrior;' probably stunned and pleased by his own success, by a reawakening '60's vibe. There do not seem to be many bad things to say about Bernie Sanders. Some say he has been slogging away in government and yet has accomplished very little and has not, until now, made much of a splash. But the people in his state do seem to love him although single payer health care failed in Vermont. I have even been tempted by Bernie. I grew up in those same energetic times when we dreamed of equality for everyone, an end to war for all people and all times and changing the "establishment" so that our government would become truly Democratic, instead of a democracy in name only. Hillary, on the other hand, seems to be no one's darling. The media rarely has anything good to say about her. They pound away at her lack of authenticity; they say that people don't like her or trust her. They say it almost every day. And some of these media folks are classified by the right as left-leaning journalists and pundits who should be allies for Hillary. "With friends like that who needs enemies.

The fact is that Hillary has not led a quiet political life. Because of her marriage to Bill Clinton, she has been in the limelight for decades. She was not just a helpmate either; she had her own career goals, and she got involved. She got her hands in the dirt, so to speak. She was not just the great lady who told the gardener what to do, she helped plant the garden. She legislated. She designed the precursor to Obama's health care plan. Hillary Clinton travelled the world and met the world's leaders.

Hillary is vulnerable to attack because she has been front and center. She has not been timid, or held back, or bided her time. She has just rolled up her sleeves and helped her nation solve its problems. She is vulnerable in so many ways because she actually "did stuff" and is accused of making wrong decisions. The tough drug arrest policy of the 1990's is the newest albatross being hung around her neck. She didn't pass that program alone. Even Bernie voted for that one. We, perhaps, only see what a mistake this policy was in hindsight.

Bernie Sanders is not looking quite so sweet these days. He is no empty suit. He has become a powerful opponent, splitting the Democratic vote and perhaps even getting some Republican votes. Independent voters find themselves choosing between Bernie Sanders and Donald Trump. How is that even possible? It boggles my mind. I see nothing in common between these two. Despite the fact that Bernie is now fighting to be President for real, he is still not getting a lot of bad press. I am even reading mixed results when it comes to vetting the plausibility of Bernie's programs. Some authors think that there is some economic viability, most have reservations.

Is Hillary as bad as the media paints her? Do the people even know anything about Hillary except what the media told us, or hinted at, or insinuated. Is Bernie as spotless and pure as the media lets him seem? I am guessing that Bernie is 'as honest as the day is long.' He just does not seem very materialistic or in possession of any strong personal ambition. While these qualities may make him a trustworthy leader, will they make him a powerful and a flexible leader? I don't think Bernie is good at compromising. I think that may be his Achilles heel. I saw the camera catch a look on Bernie's face the other day which did not look at all sweet, or flexible either. Look up "Bernie faces" on Google images. He is not always so sunny these days.

What I am saying is that Bernie Sanders is creating a split between me and other Democrats who I thought of as my allies against the Republicans and that this split has me worried. I am also worried that it is looking less like Hillary Clinton is the most viable Democratic candidate. We had better hope that if Bernie Sanders and the fans of revolution are nominated that they can actually carry the day. Will the word "socialism" be used as a club to beat Bernie up, and will the majority of American voters come to his defense? I refuse to give up on Hillary yet. We wait, we listen, we watch, we express our thoughts – but we won't know until we know.

Why We Can't Elect Donald Trump (or any of the Bully Boys) February 25, 2016

Donald J Trump could become the leader of America, but if he is elected, and if he does the things he says he will do, America will be a substantially different nation than it has always been. We can kiss our forefathers good-bye, and the high ideals they wished us to strive for as a nation. By the time we build that wall send all undocumented immigrants back to their countries of origin, build up a huge military presence and bully China, I'm not sure what America will be left with. But I think we will finally understand the word Fascism.

Older Americans shudder at the thought of a Socialist taking over our Democracy but tend to have little or no reaction when someone exhibiting signs of Fascism (Donald Trump) begins to climb in the election polls. Fascism is far more at odds with

Democracy than Socialism is but we just don't have enough understanding of what the term means for it to call forth the intensely negative visceral reaction that it should. I have written warnings about this twice before ("Megalomania, and the World", "Plague on Both Your Houses", but this time I have help from a very famous writer, Umberto Eco.

Writing from Paris, Christopher Dickey begins his article in **The Daily Beast** with this statement, "Here in Europe, people know a thing or two about fascism." He is remembering an article he read twenty years ago by the deeply philosophical Italian author Umberto Eco who died last week. "Known here in Europe, by various names – as Fascism, Nazism, Stalinism – it was the living, vibrant, vicious force that led directly to the most horrific global war in history. More recently, it took root and lingered as an active ideology in Latin America, providing a crude foundation for the repressive revolutions and dirty wars that raged from the '60's through the '80's.

Indeed, the fundamentals of fascism are with us today, in the killing fields of ISIS-land, in the madness of North Korea, and, sadly, in battered democracies from newly militaristic Japan to xenophobic, isolationist parties in Europe." And yes, in somewhat more subtle forms fascism can be found on the campaign trail in the U S of A.

Umberto Eco, in his article (title not given) gives a list of the attributes of a Fascist:

"Makes a cult of tradition
Rejects modernism
Takes action for action's sake ('thinking is a form of emasculation')
Distrust of the intellectual world
Disagreement is treason
Racist by definition ('seeks for consensus by exploiting and exacerbating the natural fear of difference')
The appeal of a frustrated middle class ('the class suffering from an economic crisis or feelings of political humiliation, and frightened by the pressure of lower social groups')
Obsession with a plot
Followers must feel humiliated ('by the ostentatious wealth and force of their enemies')
Popular elitism ('Every citizen belongs to the best people of the world, the members of the party are among the best citizens, every citizen can or ought to become a member of the party') ('the leader knows that his force is based upon the weakness of the masses; they are so weak as to need and deserve a ruler')
Life is permanent warfare ('pacifism is trafficking with the enemy')
Official heroism ('martyrdom') Machismo ('implies both disdain for women and intolerance and

condemnation of nonstandard sexual habits, from chastity to homosexuality') Selective populism ('citizens do not act, they are only called on to play the role of the People') 'Newspeak' ('from **1984**, George Orwell') ('All Nazi or Fascist schoolbooks made use of an impoverished vocabulary and an elementary syntax in order to limit
the instruments for complex and critical reasoning')"

Umberto Eco sounds like he is speaking about the Republican Party candidates and members of Congress, and especially of Donald Trump, as we know them right now, but he wrote this 20 years ago.

https://www.thedailybeast.com/articles/2016/02/22/how-umberto-eco-tagged-today-s-facists.html

I think that all the Republican candidates are unelectable, and everyone is feeling this even if they will not admit it. I am guessing that people are thinking that Donald Trump is the least dogmatic. He is not toeing the party line. He is his own man. And for some reason people cannot see the dangers in turning over our governance to this man. They want the '50's back and Donald promises the '50's. But they will return under his terms. He humiliates anyone who questions his leadership and people back down, even scary people like Ted Cruz. If we give him carte blanche to "make America great again," it will be his vision of America, not ours, and he may have a hard time ever leaving office. He may make himself President-for-life. We cannot control this man. He brooks no disagreement. In the scary GOP line-up of future Presidents perhaps the man who seems most benign is the biggest nightmare of all, but we may not know it until it is too late.

At the end of his article Dickey draws parallels with Europe then and America now. But where does Eco's 'Eternal Fascism' fit in American politics? Can it be that many of the figures parading before us in this presidential campaign year appeal to the worst instincts of "the People"? Do they play on atavistic fears and resentments, frustrations and humiliations? Are they marked by their irrationalism and anti-intellectualism, their hatred of things foreign, their desire to be seen as heroes and their gun-toting machismo?

Oh, hell yeah. But I don't need to point the finger. Umberto Eco is doing it from the grave. As he wrote more than 20 years ago:
"Franklin Roosevelt's words of November 4, 1938, are worth recalling: 'If American democracy ceases to move forward as a living force, seeking day and night by peaceful means to better the lot of our citizens, fascism will grow in strength in our land.'

"Freedom and liberation," Eco wrote, "are an unending task."

How do we get angry Americans who think any of these guys are the answer to "setting America on the right path" to understand that they will do just the opposite? How do we get Donald Trump to leave the Republican race now that all the non-scary candidates have been chased away? Getting rid of Donald is not enough. We must elect a Democrat in 2016, or American Democracy will not survive. I have no idea how we convince what I call "the pod people," brainwashed by right wing media, that they must vote against the positions they have been taught to believe in.

Stopping Donald Trump February 28, 2016

One:
I think if we want to stop Trump's big "mo" then we must fight him on his own ground. I believe a scandalous mini-series, whipped up quickly and deliciously, might do the trick. It could feature a Donald Trump-like candidate on the election trail, with flashbacks to the dirty deals and less-than-triumphant moments of his life. It could follow him everywhere – backstage at rallies and debates, in his fancy car, in his private jets, in his marriages, with his children, doing deals, talking to developers and world leaders about business, everywhere except the bathroom (because unlike Donald, we don't go there).

We could show him winning the election and then follow him into the White House (á la *House of Cards* but trashier and less subtle). We could show his policies being passed into law and the resulting unexpected reactions of Americans (even his followers) and of nations around the globe. We could show attempts to impeach him and how he resists them and grabs more power for himself, perhaps gets Congress to vote him President for Life. Really good TV script writers could get this right. Perhaps Amazon would take it on, or Netflix, or HBO or someone with access to network TV that reaches poorer Americans. Turning his own media against him may be the only way to change the minds of people who think he actually will "make America great again."

Two:
Make a series of TV ads that show President Donald in front of the UN, OPEC, US allies in the EU, and in South America, saying the things he has said in this campaign. Show film of possible reactions from famous news clips or even a movie like Evita. Show Donald in place of George Bush when the shoe is thrown, only he is taller, so he gets hit and goes down, hair in disarray. Use your mad computer skills.

Three:
I sure some of you have some interesting outside-ofthe-box ideas. Tweet them at #stopTrump

. March

The GOP War on Women and Hillary Clinton
March 2, 2016

We might not have needed Hillary Clinton if the Republicans had not spent the last seven years (at least) making women's lives miserable. Women, no matter how men feel about it, have been under attack by the GOP and especially by Conservative Evangelicals. We remember when Rush Limbaugh called Sandra Fluke a slut because she wanted to continue to have access to birth control pills. BIRTH CONTROL PILLS! I'm surprised no one recommended that clitoral mutilation should perhaps be adopted as an American rite of passage. There was an implication that women should not get any pleasure from sexual relations.

Representative Steve Pearce (R-NM) wanted women to be submissive to their husbands as a way to "fix America." Women were blamed for the demise of the families which then led to the demise of the entire social order in the US. OMG – we went to work – and we liked it. It gave some of us a sense of purpose and sometimes prevented negative female problems like frustration, depression, etc. So, the GOP told

America that "liberated" women can be blamed for
the holes in the fabric of the American Dream.

We might not have felt we had to insist on a female
President except for the number of times Congress
has tried to "defund" Planned Parenthood and
threatened in shut down the US government to do it.
We value Planned Parenthood. It has helped huge
numbers of women at times they need safe,
inexpensive, and confidential attention in their lives
for a variety of reasons (and it still does). It sort of
stands as a symbol of the freedoms women have won.
I have a tough time understanding anyone who does
not see that the GOP has been obsessed with women
and issues that should only concern women, and
perhaps their partners, ever since Obama took office.
But none of this is Obama's doing; he has no beef
with women and vice versa.

Clearly the GOP does not intend to wait until
numbers are on their side to overturn Roe v Wade
and perhaps make some forms (or all forms) of birth
control illegal. They can do this if they control all
three branches of government and there will be
almost nothing we can do to stop them. The
Republicans have created such a threat against women
that the only way we will feel safe from losing hard-
won rights, granted by law and bolstered by scientific
advances, rights that offer freedom to women, is to
put a woman in the White House. One reason many

women will support Hillary is because things look really grim for us if we don't.

The GOP has spent seven years riling up all the groups of Americans who are not white men or Evangelical women and now they act surprised that the only people in their tent are old white people, including white supremacists like David Duke and the KKK. The Republicans will reap what they sowed; we hope. The media, on the other hand, seems to have suddenly come down with collective amnesia. Hillary Clinton might rather just enjoy being a grandmother, but we can't let her do that yet. So, when the GOP starts in on Hillary, and they will, I hope that at least the women of America will remember what they stand to lose if we put a Republican in the White House.

Will We Duke it Out in the Streets?
March 13, 2016

When I listen to Ted Cruz lately, sounding like an arbiter of fairness and good grace it is too much for my civility. I watched Ted Cruz in the Senate and all along he has been the ringleader of the disrupters in Congress, stalking back and forth from the Senate to the House, sticking his big nose into Boehner's business, enforcing "purity" to a Tea Party and Evangelical agenda. He has pandered to angry white middle class Americans for the entirety of Obama's two terms in office. He has poured hate, criticism, and vituperation on Obama without ceasing. He accuses Obama of doing the things that he, Ted Cruz, is doing and no one seems to call him out on that. He does not represent many Americans, but he swears he will represent us all. Clearly, he will only represent Americans he agrees with, those who feel the same way about issues as he does.

You may say that if Ted Cruz is elected that this will be the will of the majority of the American people, but you will be wrong. The Republican Party has prepared the way for just such an extreme right-winger to win with their gerrymandering, their voter suppression, their Citizen's United, their packed Supreme Court. Ted Cruz bemoans a Supreme Court packed with liberals; while I bemoan a Supreme Court packed with the current iteration of conservatives. We are losing sight of how dangerous Ted Cruz is to America because we are presented with the even more pressing danger of a Donald Trump presidency. Ted Cruz does not, in any way, represent me. I will experience a Ted Cruz presidency as four to eight years of an America that is moving backwards. I will expect to find myself 'dangling over the pit of hell' because of some of my liberal opinions along with many other Americans.

As for the divide we saw at the Trump rally at the University of Illinois in Chicago, which was surprisingly nonviolent, Trump did not create this divide. We have watched conservatives widen a split in America that was already there, and which was exacerbated by a tough economy and by the losses of the middle class. America is divided. We are split into a white America that fears it is losing its ascendency and a minority America which might be starting to feel ready to rise. I'm not sure why everyone feels that it must be us against them. Aren't we all Americans? Don't we all want America to thrive? Conservative talk has pried away at the split in America, making it wider, driving a wedge of hate and fear into the breach. It is a reflection of the fear and racism felt at the heart of the Republican Party which has been growing increasingly less diverse and whiter. It is a party that is still reflecting the values of the old South, nursing the wounds of the Civil War, the bruised pride of the beaten Confederacy, and the authority of the supposed superiority of the old slave owners. Backward, backward, backward into a swamp of hate and remorse. Mix in righteous religious anger at the audacity of women legalizing forbidden behaviors and undermining male dominance and you have the toxic brew the Republican Party has been encouraging since Obama took office.

When we see all of the white people who the Republican Party have turned into "pod" people, mindlessly repeating Republican talking points, the bible according to Fox News, enjoying themselves at a Trump rally where they can exercise their hate and dismay without the pesky interference of other points of view, it either frightens us or delights us depending on where we stand, which side of the divide. But what we really see is that the divide is real, however it was created, no matter how much it was hyped up by Conservatives. Up until Chicago the opposition, the liberals, the young people, the Black Lives Matter movement was carefully kept out of Donald Trump's rallies. But in Chicago they organized because they had advanced notice. It is an urban area bursting with diversity and not a small Evangelical college. And there is was, staring us in the face, actually rather politely, the chasm yawning all around us between what is apparently two Americas.

If Donald Trump becomes our President and if he encourages conflict, eggs on his supporters as he has in his rallies will America see our differences boil to the surface? Perhaps papering over our animosities, constantly trying to shove them back into the crevasse is just making them stronger. Maybe we are determined to duke out our differences in the streets. I do not really think this will make us feel any better, or bring us any closer, or heal the divide. After people beat each other up there is guilt and regret and depression and wound licking not building alliances that cure and build up our nation.

We are screwed if we pick Donald Trump as our

President and we are screwed if we pick Ted Cruz. Both are too mean, too narrow-minded, too authoritarian, too self-absorbed to be able to stitch the two Americas back together into one people dedicated to making Democracy work. Neither of these men will ever be able to encourage an America that truly presents a united front to the world, an America that live outs, as well as flawed humans can, our ideals; as opposed to our fears.

Trump Demographics March 17, 2016

As Americans were watching their fortunes dwindle, their jobs disappear, their pension agreements getting rescinded, and their homes lose value or get taken back by the same corrupt banks that granted the bad mortgages – there were voices speaking in their ears, in their cars, in their man caves and media rooms blaming "others." These voices said that these beleaguered Americans were giving people who refused to work money through "entitlements" like welfare, food stamps, Medicaid and that they were wasting their money. The whispers and vein popped shouts from right-wing media claimed that giving poor people money keeps them down, turns them into dependents. Those who hammered away at middle class Americans in shock at their losses had no proof for their theory. Paul Ryan, a congressman, cited a fiction book, **Atlas Shrugged,** by Ayn Rand as proof that these takers are slackers, rather than

needy people whose children will suffer if taxpayers
harden their hearts.

If you want some other evidence, also from fiction,
and far more believable, read Charles Dickens. You
don't have to have unselfish impulses to disavow
Social Darwinism. You can be quite selfish about it
because if the poor live in squalor, that squalor affects
us all, especially our health and our mood. People
used to walk through London holding a scented
handkerchief to their noses, stepping in offal, and
even having chamber pots emptied over their heads.

Some people got sold on this short-sighted approach
to social concerns. They started to think that small
government was a good idea. After all the
government kept intruding into their lives, especially
in schools. No prayer in school was touted as the root
of all moral evil. Teaching Creationism was shouted
down by those who felt that science belongs in public
schools, religion, not so much. Christians felt they
should have the right to teach Creationism. Pundits
started to suggest that Republicans would help the
middle class get rid of social programs and turn
schools into private entities vouchered through the
states, who would allow state residents to decide on
curricula.

These disembodied voices, avidly attended to over the
air waves, eventually made their listeners aware and

incensed that minorities would be the new recipients of the American Dream. White folks said, "hell no." Keep America white. Keep America Christian. Americans speak English, they said. Eventually, the Republicans Party, not in so many words perhaps, but in code, promised that they could make it so. Even as those radio pundits graduated to TV – lo and behold, a Black man, possibly a Muslim, possibly a henchman for someone named Saul Alinsky, got elected to be the President of the United States of America!

It turns out the GOP lied. It lied to the middle class about everything. As long as Obama remained the US President, they could not deliver any of their promises. The social programs were cut but not eliminated. In fact, Obama, in stealth, in the dead of night (so the story goes) pushed through the Affordable Care Act with no Republican votes, making social health and welfare programs even bigger than ever. The government did not pass a huge school voucher program or close the Education Department which supposedly would have given states more autonomy in schools. The government doubled down on national standards and the Common Core curricula.

The Obama government did not take to Republican obstruction real well and the GOP was now in thrall to the "tea party" that coalesced because of radio whisperers. Those folks believe that America will be white again and that white America will be able to eat as much white bread as it wants. America will once again have secure factory jobs for life with pensions that are solid and generous. They believe America will stop this nonsense about fossil fuels and the environment because Big Business doesn't like it. We will build a wall so no more people can come here from Mexico without documentation and so we will not have to learn Spanish. Life will be like the 50's – we will freeze forever at a mid-century modern lifestyle – before the pill, before women's lib, before gay people, before hippies, before Civil Rights, way before 9/11. That's what the GOP was supposed to produce for their "base, and that is what the election is about, a Renaissance for white America. These are Donald Trump's people. Disappointed by America and then disappointed again by the Republicans, Donald Trump comes as close to hope that the middle class can set things straight as anyone has, and they don't really care how he does it. He seems like someone who truly could turn America into a mid-fifties theme park from sea to shining sea.

But the problem is that white America is tired, old or addicted to bad substances. White America is not the dynamic demographic it once was. We are not reproducing fast enough to prevent our numbers and prospects from dwindling. Even many of those very Republicans riding herd over Obama are ancient artifacts of distant eras (such as the 1950's). Without the energy and the thirst for freedom and success of our young immigrant groups we will very likely just turn into a fusty, dying social experiment with a Dream that was cancelled for lack of interest. A vote for Trump, or any Republican is a vote for national stagnation and decay.

Money and Hillary Clinton
March 20, 2016

In reality I know very little about Hillary Clinton and money, and neither, apparently, does anyone else, although there is plenty of theory and conspiratorial conjecturing going on out there among those who are either very informed or very paranoid. I don't know what Hillary intended in Libya, or in Africa, or in Honduras. There are many who call her the new Dick Cheney or the new Henry Kissinger and imply that she is a Machiavellian figure, or perhaps one of the Borgias.

To folks in these particular journalistic circles, she represents the very worst in American politics which has a secretive dark agenda and sends out our government officials to meddle in the business of nations around the world, build nations up and tear nations down, all for cynical reasons having to do with economics and money. Or perhaps Hillary has no mission to inform her actions but is simply acting on her own. According to these folks Hillary is a sinister figure who ruins nations when their economies are getting too successful and are challenging the American economy. Wow! Who knew Hillary was this powerful and this corrupt? Apparently, everyone but me.

Bernie Sanders indicts Hillary for using government service to get rich. He tells his supporters anecdotes which supposedly prove that she has offered influence in return for donations from wealthy nations. Sanders apparently implies that the Clinton Foundation is a front to peddle influence and line the Clinton's pockets. He believes that accepting money from Wall Street proves that you are absolutely corrupt. His followers believe all this is true beyond a shadow of a doubt and they revile Hillary for this. Again, I did not ascribe to Hillary even this level of villainy. They say that Hillary is a criminal who should be indicted for war crimes, or crimes against humanity, or bribery, or if nothing else sticks, then for the private email server thing (possibly risking national security). How naïve am I? I see that half of Congress is made up of millionaires, many of whom lined their bank accounts while in government service. I know that Bernie Sanders is solidly against money in politics, feeling that it robs the people of their right to govern. I agree with him. I was shocked when Citizens United was upheld by the Supreme Court, giving legitimacy to all the money that floods into politics in Washington. But Hillary came up as a politician operating within the system we have now. Bernie is a revolutionary who wants to dump the system we have now. We could possibly get money out of politics through a grassroots groundswell, but it is more likely that it will be a tough slog, accomplished in baby steps.

Hillary, as the first woman to get this close to being an America President, has a foot in the past and a foot in the future. She cannot be blamed for playing the game according to the rules of the boy's club. We are always changing the rules just when a woman arrives at a threshold. Bernie's purity did not help him shine in Congress, although it certainly looks appealing now. But there is no other person in our government like Bernie Sanders and changing the way our government does business cannot be as easy as he makes it sound. If Donald Trump is dividing the nation before he gains the office, Bernie Sanders is likely to divide it if he becomes our President. People who have been on the gravy train for years are not going to gently step aside. If we the people win the day if might be worth the fight, but we could probably win the day eventually with just good solid strategy if we had a plan.

I believe that people are painting Hillary as a villain based on some convoluted reasoning and theorizing. Of course, if anyone can prove these accusations beyond any doubt then I suppose that Hillary is too byzantine to make a good President. If she actually treats the globe like some kind of calculated game of Risk then that is diabolical and she should be stopped. I just don't buy it.

Who's to Blame?
March 24, 2016

I'm sure that the blame game is played during every election season, and, in fact, it appears that it is a perennial political favorite, election year or not. Sometimes politicians place blame to distract attention away from the responsibilities their own party bears for some domestic or foreign situation. In the 2016 election it is quite maddening and entertaining to watch Republicans place the blame on the Obama administration for things that we have been blaming on George W. Bush. Should we blame Bush or ISIS or is Obama to blame?

Well, there is truth in the cosmic wisdom that all things are interconnected and if you are a Republican it only takes about 85 steps to get from the argument that places the blame on Bush for the Iraq War to blaming Obama. You just have to say over and over that ISIS formed because Obama is weak, or because he used drone strikes, or because he took the troops out of Iraq too soon, or any number of different imagined flaws in the Obama government.

But all the razzle-dazzle reasoning that links Obama to ISIS is just a ploy to hopefully make us forget the much more seminal role that Bush and the GOP played in destabilizing the Middle East. Republicans hope that enough time has passed to convince most Americans that Obama is the one we should be angry with and that the only possible conclusion we can draw is to elect a Republican. The GOP believes, I think, that most Americans have the attention span of gnats. The blame game is so useful exactly because it can cause confusion even in those who were once certain they knew who was responsible.

Today I read an article that blamed elitist Democrats for the rise of Donald Trump. You might guess that it took more than a few logical jumps to accomplish that feat of pretzel reasoning. The gist of the argument is that the Democratic Party elites did not back up the middle class when the corporations left, when the free trade agreements were passed, when the unions destroyed the marketplace by asking for ever higher salaries and benefits, when people lost their jobs and their pensions. Instead, the Democrats voted in favor of free trade agreements which hurt the American middle class and did not continue to support the regulations on Wall Street. The contention of this author was that the Democrats share with the Republicans the responsibility for Trump because they abandoned the middle class and the middle class has, in retribution, abandoned them.

It's creative, but is it true? Surprisingly this article is from *The Daily Kos* which usually leans far left.

Obviously there seems to be enough culpability so that everyone can be tarnished in the blame game. But probably if blame must be assigned at all, the bulk of it should go to the group or individual that is connected by the straightest lines. If you have to jump through too many hoops to follow the blame trail, then we are back in "everything is interconnected" territory.

There are always lessons to be learned though from events or situations that are serious enough that they lead us to look around for someone to saddle with any give mess. In the case of what happened in the wake of the Iraq War and in the case of what is going on in the 2016 election, placing blame correctly has everything to do with who should win the election, although not necessarily who will win the election. So, both parties look around to place the burden of blame on the other party or on the President or on anyone they can think of if they want to confuse voters. As a voter I can say that they succeed somewhat in arguing that day is night and that the guilty party is not who we always thought it was. By the time the politicians and the media are done with the blame game we begin to question even the events we lived through. The resulting brain tangle is one of the reasons many people hate elections and just decide that they will not vote at all. Be vigilant. Don't let politicians playing the blame game stop you from voting. You can always fall back on that old school saying, "your first thought is best."

April

If You Are Not in the Game, Get Out of the Way April 1, 2016

There is only one entrance to the field of play. It is a narrow opening in a board-and-glass wall. On the field inside the wall, there is a lop-sided version of the game being played badly by two unequal teams. The additional players needed on the field want to help their teammates, but the other team is blocking the opening. They have been blocking for a long time – game after game. The team that won the toss is not able to put their game plan into action. The game has never been stalled in quite this way before. This is, of course, a symbolic game.

However, what happens in the real game affects real people in an entire nation, in fact, in the whole world. And yet the entrance to this game which we call government has been blocked for almost eight years. The team that is supposed to be receiving has bent the rules. They have cheated to get such a lop-sided game. They plan to stop the game until they win the toss and control the action once again. Sound familiar? This is what the Republican Party has been doing. The first two years of Obama's first term were mainly spent cleaning up Bush's economic mess. The GOP's strategies in the media (Talk Radio, Fox) and their shenanigans in the states with redistricting and ALEC allowed them to control the House.

Between 2010 and 2012 Republicans blocked Obama and, for all practical purposes brought our government to a standstill. They turned a strategy invented by Dennis Hastert into a rule to block legislation in the House and they used the filibuster to block bills in the Senate. In 2012 their gerrymandering, their propaganda, their billionaires, and their control over state governments allowed them to gain a majority in both the House and the Senate.

Federal judges were overwhelmingly Conservative, and this Conservative Congress blocked most Liberal court nominations. The Supreme Court was a bit less skewed, but still tended towards the right.

The fact that a party can skew the courts on purpose was known, but never used in such a bold fashion. This ability to stop government in order to keep your party in power forever is a terrible loophole and we can't keep such a sneaky coup from happening then our government, as we know it, may dissolve. The

GOP has hollowed out the US Constitution. I don't want us to forget this as we head into this election. We never experienced the full measure of Obama's agenda. We will never know what would have happened to the American economy if Obama got to carry out his policies. Republicans kept America from being able to test out the approaches that Democrats wanted to use to engender growth. What if we had said yes to a bit of liberal spending instead of the GOP's hypocritical austerity (after all the GOP crashed the economy to begin with)? We have experienced the most hobbled version of Obama's agenda imaginable. The GOP used up Obama's time and our tax dollars voting to overturn the Affordable Care Act over 60 times, voting to defund Planned Parenthood again and again (which is not even possible without getting rid of Medicaid), taking food stamps away from poor people, and shutting down the government. They would not allow infrastructure spending, they invited Netanyahu to address Congress (Obama was not welcome), 47 senators signed a letter to the leaders of Iran in an attempt to undermine Obama's hard-fought negotiations.

Please remember these things when you go to the polls in November. We got to look at Obama's nice face, but we hardly saw any of his policies put into effect. For eight years we have been following the Republican agenda. We don't need to elect them to see what their America will be like. I think we would

be feeling more prosperous if they had not blocked
Obama and the left, and I think we need to have a
do-over without the obstruction.

Turn the Senate around, elect another Democratic
President, and let the left lead for at least the next
four years and I believe that you will see America
return to good fiscal health and remain, for the most
part, at peace with a chaotic and changing world. If
you believe that the past eight years represent the
outcomes of a liberal agenda, widely applied as policy,
then you are misguided, and you have been misled on
purpose. Stop watching Fox News.

Who Will End Obstructionism?
April 10, 2016

I will fight for Hillary Clinton right to the end,
whenever that is. I do think women can do as well in
the Presidency as men have done. I am tired of
women being expected to wait until some perfect
moment which of course will never arrive. There are
no perfect moments. Even Obama's seemingly
perfect moment was ruined by racism and
obstruction. If we get Bernie, I will be fine with that,
but I have to stay in the fight.

The only question that bugs me is which of these two
will be able to bring back regular order to Congress,

to send the "teabaggers" packing and the Evangelicals out to do good works? The Conservatives hate Hillary possibly even more than they loathed the idea of an Obama Presidency. Their hate has become rabid and personal. Will we have four to eight more years of obstruction and hate speech, this time against women? Will they just vote over and over to impeach her? There could be 60+ more votes against the ACA. How many more votes will there be to defund Planned Parenthood? More of this will not be good for America. It will not be good for the world, although perhaps it is emotional baggage we must sort through. Does Hillary have a plan to change things just in case we don't win some seats back in the Senate?

Can Bernie defuse and render harmless the Conservative push to pursue every policy that would be harmful to America? He certainly understands what is harmful about the right-wing agenda and he will hold the line against any progress towards the Conservative way. But will he also be unable to breach the obstructive moves of a party that owns 30 state governments, both houses of Congress, and the courts? Will it help that he pushes Republican buttons by pursuing policies that are far outside their ken? Will he blow them to smithereens when he moves to break up the banks and rein in Wall Street? Will revolutionary zeal be better than the strategies of someone who knows everyone and who knows her way around the politics of DC? Or will there just be two revolutionary groups in a war of words?

Is there any candidate the Democrats could have put forth who could "treat with" today's GOP? If a Democrat wins the Presidency and the obstruction continues will the people finally get involved? Will we the people insist that it is not OK to go to Congress if it is your intention to hold the American government hostage until it does what Republicans want? It is troubling that we cannot see into the future and know who would be able to make headway in America right now against the misguided and unenlightened mess that is today's GOP. We can, though, and we should certainly contribute to the movements by the Democrats to change as many seats in Congress as possible in 2016. Emily's List tries to get Democratic women elected. If you contribute to the DNC, the dollars get spread around. Even Hillary donates some of her dollars to down ballot elections and Bernie is talking about doing that.

The people's dollars are stretched thin by all the causes that need our contributions to fight for right, but at this moment, winning the election must be a top priority. You don't have to contribute much because small donations grow very big when millions of people contribute, and there are often richer donors who match or multiply small donations. Think of it as creating a war chest in case we need it.

Global Concerns
April 12, 2016

It is difficult to watch the strife and human abuse that we see daily on our planet, but it seems, at least on a global scale, that is all we can do. We have seen the consequences of meddling, or even just trying to tweak the progress of those who seem to have "right" on their side, those who seem to promise the best outcomes for their own people and everyone else on our world. And we have seen the fallout from trying to wreck those who seem to promise the worst outcomes.

We want to bridge the differences in the Middle East, we want to feed starving people (everywhere except in America it sometimes seems), we want to open up North Korea and reunite the North with the South, we want to be rid of crazy megalomaniacal leaders, we want some economic parity across nations and within nations so as to produce an income for each person that meets and exceeds basic needs. We are told that small acts of mercy are not too intrusive, but stepping in like some kind of overlord, however benign is not acceptable and more often than not has unintended consequences and possibly unconscious, but astonishingly selfish motive.

So what does a person do as s/he watches, as if
human events are some kinds of spectator sport, the
parade of inhuman behavior which surrounds us
(think of that awfully amazing Bosch painting, 'The
Garden of Earthly Delights'). We try to intervene
gently here and nudge events there and stop, if at all
possible, the worst of the horrors, while repulsing any
attempt to bring the mayhem to our side of the globe.

After all, we have our own internal concerns to attend
to, our own problems to solve and we cannot even
choose between some kind of self-interested tough
love and good old-fashioned human compassion.
Half of us want the Industrial Age back and half of us
are looking to see what the future will bring, and we
hope it is something less materialistic, less
backbreaking and less harmful to the planet.

While it is tempting to turn inward and wall out the
rest of the world, we know in our guts that it is
impossible. We would just atrophy in a kind of
unproductive inbreeding that would eventually
destroy us. Injections of new energy are ever more
necessary as the temptation to stagnate and rusticate
grows stronger.

We hold before us, in the chemical pathways of our
brains a gleaming future where technology enfolds
and surrounds us (perhaps also separates us), a sort of
engineer-centric future in which governance is settled

(although quite possible quite ponderous) and ingenuity is the "coin of the realm." The planet still has dark places and sad corners and back alleys, but the main thrust is towards a mechanics that will propel us outward from this too tiny, destined-for-extinction planet, out into the vastness of the universe or universes, one human colony at a time. (What terrible imperialism will be practiced depends on whether the universe is populated by others or exist just for our expansion.) We call it Space, and it is the only future we can imagine that gives scope to our restless adventurous spirit and our insatiable need to know.

We are not ready to occupy all that beckoning Space right now. We are earthbound on this beloved planet to either learn to survive this present chaos or not. So we watch. We watch the upheavals here on Earth. Is it just growing pains? Is it the beginnings of a better future? Will it resolve in decades, or will it take centuries? Or will it be back to the Dark Ages, reboot, start over after whatever annihilation we perpetrate on each other?

Some people don't want the world's leaders to have a vision of a global future. They believe it betrays America to discuss some kind of orderly progression towards a more peaceful, and yet still free, global society. They believe the plan that exists (if there is one) gets rid of nations (in other words, gets rid of

America) in favor of some kind of world government, and world military, world police force, and global social structure. They want the future of the world to be an American future. They want America to govern the world (a prospect that is not looking at all doable right now seeing that we cannot even decide how to govern ourselves). I also harbor a desire to have the whole world become an American world. This is the nature of chauvinism. I think I could let this incarnation of America go if I thought a global government would strive for the same ideals. A global government seems almost as distant a goal as populating Space.

We may be able to sit back and watch the rest of the world as if through a VR headset, but we will not be able to keep our hand off world events in every case. We will be inspired to push here, prod there, rescue when necessary and if possible. This is a very difficult position we are in right now. I doubt we can maintain our distance for long. These is a cycle to this kind of seemingly omnipresent upheaval, I think, but are we at the low point or the high point? In the meantime, we still need, at the very least, to call attention to atrocity wherever and whenever we see it. I think that it helps us to stop amid all the myriad detailed problems to be addressed to step back and picture a hopeful future and to take a wide view at the entire world of human endeavor and possibility.

Sad That We Can't Discuss Politics April 19, 2016

Today I went to the post office, and I ended up being there for quite a while because I used the wrong envelope and I had to start over. I let people go ahead of me but by the time I finished my new envelope the line had not moved at all. Someone was getting a passport, apparently a very exacting and time-consuming task. If you ever get behind someone filling in passport paperwork and having it checked over you might as well leave, do another errand, and then come back. There was one other clerk, but she had an Aussie gentleman with very complicated insurance and packing issues. So, we stood in line. (At least we had a counter to lean on.) We began to discuss our pets who are, apparently, all spoiled rotten.

As our wait continued, we began to discuss the conditions that were keeping us waiting. I was nice and did not try to make anyone feel too badly. The man next to me in line knew that the desk was one clerk short because the missing clerk was his wife. She had a vacation day. We were pleasant and civil, just chatting. But it was primary day, so I mentioned my anxiety as I waited to find out the results of the voting. I mentioned that I was looking forward to seeing Hillary Clinton win the New York primary. I was hoping people would pipe up and say who they would like to see win.

I know that politics is not a topic that is supposed to be discussed in polite company. But I, of course, can't help myself. I wanted to know what people were thinking on this primary day. Sadly, I believe it has become more difficult for us to discuss politics than ever. We should at least be able to talk about what we think we know about the candidates and where we got our information.

However, as soon as I said Hillary's name a woman down the line made a sour face and said Hillary is a liar. Now I don't think this woman knows Hillary personally and I could not really ask where the woman was from, although she had accent, but as soon as I said Hillary's name she made that disapproving prune face. If she came from another country maybe Hillary did something there that had upset her. After all, Hillary was the Secretary of State. I tried to probe gently, because I couldn't accept an insult without some kind of backup, but the woman just repeated that Hillary s a liar.

Perhaps Hillary Clinton is a liar, after all 'everyone' says she is, but in my mind, since I was too intimidated to attempt any more conversation, I just tried to argue that the only way we know about Hillary is through the media and that it is always important to consider the slant of any particular media that is supposedly offering evidence against Hillary. When I have traced many of the "proofs" back to their source I have found the media to be right- wing media. I would bet that the main source of news for this woman is Fox News. I will never know if that is true though.

The woman made an instant decision to dislike me because I had an opinion about Hillary Clinton that did not agree with hers. I would have loved to listen to the reasons why she had concluded that Hillary is a liar. I would have loved to share my reasons why I do not believe Hillary to be quite the monster that the media paints her. But the conversation was over, and it was over with rancor on the part of one of us and dismay on the part of the other. Everyone else in that long post office line (we were there for about half an hour) said not one peep either during or after the exchange.

I can't help thinking that it is sad that we can't talk politics at all in our free society, at least with anyone whose opinions differ from ours. People have chosen their favored media outlet and are not the least bit curious about what other media outlets have to say. We no longer take in all sides and try to make sense of all the evidence. We make up our mind and any attempt to offer another point of view meets with a stone wall of anger and defensiveness. I know this has probably been true of every society from time to time when passions run high and answers are tough to come by, but it's a shame and I hope such inflexibility disappears and that we will be able to try to analyze and decide important cultural matters with some sophistication and a spirit of mediation at some point in the near future.

I Blame Donald Trump
April 26, 2016

Donald Trump has changed the 2016 primaries in so many ways. He has been like *deus ex machina* who popped up in an enormous list of GOP characters with little to differentiate one from the next. He did not fit the mold, but he was no more acceptable to me than any other Republican. I didn't think I could be shocked after six years of disrupters in Congress making ignorant suggestions to women that would set the culture back 50 years if heeded. I was afraid when the Supreme Court did not uphold the most essential section of the voting rights act, the requirement that certain states get clearance before changing their voting laws, but still, I did not foresee how quickly the states would "celebrate" their "freedom" by repressing votes. Watching states break the law in respect to Roe v Wade by imposing bogus rules to close clinic after clinic seemed quite shocking enough, especially when courts backed them up. I expected the courts to say, "whoa Nellie" (because that's the way these guys talk – remember the one who recommended that women practice birth control by putting an aspirin between their knees and keeping their knees closed around it.) The courts did nothing. That's when I realized how many Conservative judges had been appointed in the courts in many of our states.

I could go on, but my point is actually that Donald Trump managed to drive my "no they didn't" reaction up several more notches. His remarks about Mexicans, about the "wall," about China, deporting undocumented immigrants, Megan Fox, about women in general, about Muslims – well, you were there – you heard it. Then there was his apparent comfort with a physicality that we usually avoid in American politics. We initially use our words. His behavior made the shock waves of the Republican heresies over the past six years pale by comparison.

As we know the other Republican candidates did not seem any happier with Donald's injection of himself into an already crowded race. He had been a Democrat. Conservatives who had been making a big point about GOP purity tests had to move over and include this famous person who had certainly not been tested for purity. And he was winning, pulling large crowds, taking up all the space on a 24/7 media that usually could be captured only temporarily by a particularly audacious act. Ted Cruz had attempted frequent newsworthy nonsense, but Donald did it practically nonstop. However, Trump has also served as a sort of buffer between the Democratic primary race and the rest of the Republican slate, getting picked off one by one before our incredulous eyes. We expected to worry about Scott Walker and Ted Cruz and Jeb Bush, but instead every eye and ear was on Donald. For the most part, Hillary and Bernie were left alone to run their own race.

Trump's presence in the race has also allowed Ted Cruz to take up the second position on the GOP side. He expects an open convention, and he expects the coveted Republican nomination to eventually fall to him. I have watched Ted Cruz throughout the Obama administration, and he made me very worried right from the first time I set eyes on him. In fact, I wrote an article called "Ted Cruz: Sinister or Cartoonish" about my initial observations.

I have predicted to myself that somehow he would "worm" his way into the White House and I have tried to speak out against this whenever possible. He is closer to the White House than he has ever been. He is intelligent, if inflexible, and he is strategic. He believes he is a genius. As geniuses go, I can think of several I would prefer over him. If Donald had not inserted himself into the primary would Cruz have made it this far? I don't know, of course, no one does. But if I end up with Ted Cruz as my President in

2017, I will blame Donald. Who will I blame if we end up with Donald Trump in the White House? I will blame the Democrats. Hillary, there is a lot resting on your shoulders because if you win the nomination, we are counting on you to beat the chosen one of these two guys and Donald has sort of fogged up everyone's view. Ted Cruz is advancing almost under the radar, a stealth campaign.

Donald Trump's Way Back Foreign Policy Machine
April 28, 2016

It is dangerous to listen to someone like Donald Trump whose nostalgia date (his way-back time machine) is set to the 60's and 70's. No problem if you're just telling stories to your grandchildren but a "huge" problem if you are the President of the. United States. Donald's idea of winning – he said in his foreign policy speech – is our victory in WWII, and he also gives America credit for winning the Cold War. Donald is another worshipper of the only "perfect" American President, Ronald Reagan. He likes an America that is pugilistic and muscular.

Trump believes we haven't won a war since World War Two or the Cold War because we have been weak. He, perhaps, would have liked Ronald Reagan to be made President for Life. Alzheimer's, sadly, would have put the kibosh on that. However, except for Saint Ronald (who if you studied real history was way less than perfect) no one else has measured up. According to Trump the weakest leader of all has been President Obama (who is never given the honorific) and Hillary Clinton will be just as bad. But what Donald Trump, stuck in the old days, cannot see is that the very philosophy concerning the ways we participate in the world has evolved.

We have learned not to go to war lightly – well no we haven't but we, at least are not turning every skirmish into a world war, or every power-hungry man into an existential threat (OK, we're not perfect at that either but we're trying). We have learned that nation building in far-flung corners of the globe is expensive and not often appreciated or even successful, which doesn't mean we will refrain. We surely have had plenty of examples of the totally unforeseen consequences of regime change, although from time to time we still can't seem to resist. We especially can't help injecting ourselves into the chaos in the nations of our nearest neighbors, often with horrifying results.

Donald wants to bring this all back along with torture and secrecy and threats (even nukes). So, while evidence suggests that tactics that we and others have used in the past will not actually make America great again, that the only thing resorting to these old military chestnuts can do is enhance our reputation as "ugly Americans," Donald Trump, still stuck in the post-World War II glow, seems unaware of such evidence.

Trump blames Obama and Clinton for the "the confusion, chaos, and disarray" in the world but many of us believe that the Bush administration opened the Pandora's Box that has turned into the seething, painfully transitioning Middle East we see and deal with today. Whether the region tried to shake off their authoritarian leaders, or whether the Iraq War had a domino effect, or whether Americans had a hand in their fall from power, it is clear that the Middle East does not have a tradition of democratic rule and that is not the setting it reboots to. Perhaps we need to flood the area with reasons to join the developed world that make sense in relation to Muslim beliefs.

However, I contend that we are actually at the point where war and the environment meet, because if we cannot work across nations, and stay somewhat peaceful and stable as the inhabitants of this planet we may be doomed. If we can't work efficiently as caretakers and help create a sustainable lifestyle for the exploding population, then confusion, chaos and disarray will be the order of the day, every day. Old imperialists and militaristic strategies may have once made America feel large and in charge, but these outdated attitudes towards our global neighbors, however un-neighborly, are not what we need now.

We could go with America First and decide, as we see our planet become a less hospitable place to live, to build those walls and annihilate our enemies (or be annihilated, because people fight back). That's one way to be sustainable, wipe out anyone who won't accept our leadership. But where is the challenge in that? It is far more interesting to try to design global strategies that will give everyone a livable spot in a world exhibiting rapid climate change. It is far more intelligent to keep striving to colonize other planets than to turn this one into a radioactive nuclear wasteland.

Earth probably doesn't care if we take care of it; it will live on without us. But if we want the Earth to support human life we may need to start cooperating soon now. We can't just take a boilerplate set of old war policies and rely on them to keep the flaws in human nature from sucking us under. The nations who understand the risks to our planet need to be strong, yes, but also cooperative, creative and nuanced; and we need a global design for where we would like things to go here on Earth – and for that we need peace, not warmongering. The reason Donald Trump's foreign policies, and in fact the foreign policy stances of the Republican Party are dangerous is because they will not meet current and future needs of Americans or anyone else on Earth.

May

Desert Dwellers and Polar Ice Caps
May 1, 2016

How do we get desert dwellers to care that the polar ice caps are melting. We can't even get Republicans who can see what is happening in Norfolk and Miami to pay attention. When you live in a dry, hot part of the world and you are bent on conquest or survival it is difficult to remember that everything is interconnected, even if some of your best oil wells are located near coastlines. How do you get a terrorist caught up in bringing back the 14 th century to look over his shoulder and see the tsunami in his future? Republicans, if they entertain the notion of climate change at all, refuse to accept that it is caused by human activities. We know why they do this, investments and power structures. If we find alternatives to fossil fuels, they fear that their bank accounts will dwindle. They cannot accept that the age of fossil fuels, and, in fact, the Industrial Age is ending. They are starving poorer Americans, hoarding all the money on purpose. Of course, they enjoy being rich, but you can only buy so many homes and yachts. Their real aim is to recreate 1890's America when there were no worker's rights, no unions, no minimum wage requirements and no regulations on businesses.

You cannot get factories back to America if workers expect to get paid thirty or forty dollar an hour. You have to get them down around two dollars an hour. No wonder the GOP hates the movement for a $15 minimum hourly wage. If you add addiction into the no-minimum-wage mix, we get to the bottom even faster. Furthermore, if you think that humans have played no role in climate change then you can claim that, ergo, there is nothing humans can do to stop such changes and you can carry on blithely with your plan for a fossil-fuel-based master/serf economy. Take all the people's toys away and make them climb that ladder of opportunity all over again – an Industrial Age do-over.

I know there are those who will say that we have to still have factories, we have to still produce things and, of course, we always will, but it does not take hundreds of workers to run a modern factory. The application of robotics is setting people free of work and creating new problems because then we have no alternative productive role to offer them.

Some may decide to be academics, but not everyone can or will choose that route. We really need to work on the roles societies will provide for people who are not needed to do work, or we need to find work they will feel good about doing. The American work ethic works against this. Rich folks get all huffy about people who don't have a reason to, or skill set for work. In America those who work labor for longer hours with shorter vacations than almost any other developed nation. There must be a better goal for Americans who are not wealthy than working for the Future Taskmasters of America. I have heard people trying to start a back-to-the-farm movement, but farming was not as romantic a lifestyle as it is in memory. Just read **One Thousand Acres** by Jane Smiley.

How do we get rich people – Capitalist "pigs" as we used to call them – on board to prepare Earth for the 9 billion people who will live on it by 2050? Without their help, with their very active opposition, it is a push-pull operation and basically a wash. Progress is in baby steps when we need giant ones. How do we get megalomaniacs intent on power to tune into anything except their own selfish drive for fame, or historical relevance, or whatever when they may just be, at base, mad men. Without China, without Russia, without the Middle East or Africa who is left to work on this truly existential threat – in the sense of a threat to human survival?

Are humans worth fighting to save or should we just let extinction happen to a species that has proven to be a bit too rapacious to coexist peacefully anywhere. And as for the idea that freedom alone should be attractive to people in every nation, I do not think that we are setting a very good example for the ways in which freedom makes life wonderful. In fact, sometimes our notion of freedom makes it impossible to impose an organizational global design that might help us meet future needs.

There are no walls in the ocean (well, except by the Netherlands) so one body of water hits every nation with a coastline. Bodies of water within nations such as rivers and lakes will eventually rise also. We don't need more salt water. The world will need a lot of fresh water for those 9 billion people. Water levels are just one outcome of polar melting. It is easy to foresee fear and anger growing as changes occur to geography and crowded coastal cities. It is easy to foresee tempers on edge and fights breaking out. Unless we are proactive and devise strategies to deal with negative human interactions, apocalyptic scenes may be as common in the near future as natural disasters are becoming in the present.

Getting people, made ever suspicious of conspiracy, by those who oppose change, worried about losing freedom or losing comfort, to create any sort of "matrix" of leadership that can ameliorate chaos seems almost impossible to imagine. Our war/peace dynamic may be so hard-wired into us that we will continue to fight our way right through climate change and beyond (if there is a beyond). We surely need some heroes and heroines who disregard the worst in humanity to save the best in humanity if we are to survive the population explosion and simultaneous climate change. If thinking about these things does not convince people that war is an obsolete and primitive construct, then I don't know what will.

However, the militants will not stop their crusades for some probably unreachable ideal to give space to find a solution to issues of climate crisis. It is the human condition to strive for a cultural equality and religious purity or a manifest destiny that will, most likely, never exist. So, the question becomes one of finding a way to keep the weaponized bickering at bay while also creating a new schema for a crowded planet that is at an environmental tipping point. I am afraid that I doubt that this will ever happen.

Jimmy Kimmel did a You Tube on the subject:

https://youtube.com/watch?v=9UCdFbyL8yo

June

Bernie Flaws
June 5, 2016

I am always talking about what imperfect beings people are. If you're a believer then it goes right back to those two original forebears of ours, Adam and Eve. They could have left us full of blissful ignorance and innocence but they were weak and so we have dual natures. Each one of us holds the paradoxes within us, in differing proportions, because of so many variables like our nurture in childhood, the social circumstances into which we are born, the cultural context that surrounds us during our relatively short lives.

We hold strengths and at the same time weaknesses, we are good, and we are bad, we have talents and things that we seem to have little skill for, we are both stable and unstable at times, happy and depressed, healthy and unhealthy, brilliant and dumb all mixed in an infinite array that makes each one of us unique in spite of our similarities. If you are not a believer, it is almost enough to make you believe that the Christian origin story holds more than a kernel of truth. Or we are just made this way?

What we also know to be true is that all our actions, our inventions, our discoveries, and our endeavors hold the same human paradoxes within them; that they can be used for good or for evil, that they can make our lives worse or better. We know that a flawed human can twist anything to evil purposes or a human with better motives or character can act from strength and get positive results from the same event, invention, idea or strategy. Nuclear energy is probably our clearest example of this – used benignly it can provide power to run the devices that make our lives more comfortable – used as a weapon it can wipe out cities.

We get this stuff on a cosmic level, but we also understand that these same paradoxes operate in our daily lives, so I accept and perhaps you do also that Hillary Clinton is both experienced and flawed. I accept that she made a mistake choosing a private server, if only because it gave her many enemies an opening to argue that she was either planning to have a way to hide information, or that she is capable of making bad choices, both things we don't really look for in a person running for President of the United States. However, all Presidents make mistakes given the complex issues they deal with minute to minute. Sometimes we get a leader who seems to make brilliant decisions, but we usually don't know that until we get some historical perspective on their legacy. And from the distance offered by time we are able to see that mistakes were also made.

However, it seems that people have difficulty seeing the flaws that Bernie Sanders might have. His message is so consistent and has been for so many years that he seems steady and dedicated. Recent events reveal that Bernie Sanders is starting to show the ways in which his very strengths might also be his weaknesses. Bernie is showing himself to be a bit compulsive these days. He does not seem to be terribly flexible.

He cannot seem to show us the practical details that will allow him to effectively change things in Washington and in America. How does he plan to win new rights for workers? How does he plan to rein in Wall Street without tanking our already hobbled economy? How will he find the money for strengthening benefits? Can he raise the taxes on the wealthy? In almost every area we need to change the way wealth moves in America and the need for fairness to equalize privilege. It makes sense to us but Bernie Sanders has not really spelled out how he intends to get us there. So his message may be all to the good, but his vagueness and the way his specifics are sort of stored in the "cloud" and inaccessible may not be all to the good.

And again, I suggest that Bernie Sanders is almost coming off a bit obsessive-compulsive lately. He said he would have a fifty-state strategy, which is fine, but he doesn't seem inclined or able to make adjustments for the good of the Democratic Party. I suppose if you are staging a Revolution you need to be a revolutionary, not someone who compromises. But do Bernie's defensiveness and his meanness actually resulting from an inability to be flexible, to have a certain degree of political nimbleness? He has remained true to socialist principles for so many decades while America wanted nothing to do with socialism.

Personally, I do not believe that socialism is necessary in a democracy because government is already of the people, by the people, and for the people. Where I do agree with Bernie is when he recounts how far away we are from a true democracy. It is not socialism I fight for; it is democracy. In a democracy you don't need socialism because we are the people, and we take care of all the people. But if our democracy is becoming, or has already become, an oligarchy, then Mr. Sanders is right in arguing that the people (all of the people) need to take back their government and that this will probably mean making money talk less and every vote count more. However, we must accept that if rich folks take their money out of government, which they have shown a willingness to do, there may be fewer things our government can do for 'we the people.'

But what really bothers me is how Bernie Sanders has seemed more and more like a curmudgeon lately, so intent on his own business that he barely notices what is going on around him. He does not admonish Donald Trump in any sustained way for his outrageous pronouncements and astonishingly unevolved policies. He does not raise money for down-party candidates (except that he did find three worthy souls). He fights with Democratic Party leaders and threatens to bring revolution to the Democratic Convention. He has a right to do these things, but they are not done in a manner that suggests strength and composure. They are done with old man bitterness and complaints about bad rules and stacked decks. Instead of sounding like an eventual winner, he just sounds like a sore loser. Bernie Sanders does have flaws and lately he is showing them to us almost every day. If you're planning to vote for him because you think he is Mr. Wonderful, then I guess you won't have noticed that he is just looking like Mr. Ticked Off.

Celebrating Hillary and History
June 12, 2016

Bear with me while I do a little celebration of one historical bit of progress made here in June of 2016. We have just managed to win enough votes in the primary for a woman to become the presumptive nominee of a major political party, the Democrats, of course. It is probably difficult for some of you to understand, as we perhaps come at this from different perspectives of age, gender, political persuasion, but to have this happen in my lifetime is even better than flying cars (although I saw a great one the other day on Facebook).

"YIPPEE" (Sorry, that just slipped out.)

We have been one of the most backward nations in this regard, perhaps because some of our men (and a surprising number of them are Republican) think they are alpha dogs, and they don't like to give up any power. Not wanting to give up power, however, can also be a sign that the of strength of these men does not run deep, that they cannot play a supportive role. The need to dominate makes them seem unsure of their place, and that they must be constantly on the offensive. I guess they don't see that this makes them look defensive and weak. Please do not accuse me of lumping all men into one category. I see lots of healthy and evolved men who are loving, supportive, and not at all threatened by women who are good leaders. They just don't seem to be in Congress right now.

"I'M SO EXCITED…" (Oops, a hiccup.)

I ask you to bear with me if you wanted Bernie Sanders as our next President (although it sounds like he may still be calling for "the revolution" to win the day in this regard). Bernie doesn't look like a leader of a revolt to me right now, just someone who can't accept when he has lost. I have faith that Bernie Sanders will see some of his wishes for the people fulfilled; but he lost, so I doubt he will get total satisfaction unless there truly is a revolution, or the super delegates do a 180-degree turn.

Bernie taught us something very important. He taught us that you can run for office without being a millionaire/billionaire if you understand the needs of the people and if you can project your message with power and authenticity. He taught us that there are ways to get big money out of politics, that we don't need that Citizens United v FEC decision or the deliberate avoidance of any laws to control dark money in politics. This is an area that is ripe for reform, and I hope that it is something Hillary will tackle after she wins in November.

"SO NOT MEH!"

I also ask you to let me have my mini-celebration now, which I hope will turn into a great big one in November because I know that Hillary Clinton is not everyone's cup of tea. The people who become leaders by catching a wave of a moment in history when their beliefs, experiences, character traits, or passions are resonating are never perfect. Some are beloved, some are not. Some grow on us, some don't. Apparently, a few of those suffragettes were slightly insufferable. So is Hillary to some of you, although I think the women at least should be more sympathetic and understand the sacrifices Hillary had to make to get to this historical position she has just arrived at.

She was not born to a wealthy family, although she and Bill did find affluence in politics and law (which many see as suspicious, a proof of unethical practices). She went through the same struggles as any mother in those days torn between staying home to raise and enjoy a child or pursuing a career, especially a high-powered career with a grueling schedule. Chelsea seems to have turned out just fine and is still close to both her mom and her dad, perhaps a sign that Hillary and Bill hit the right balance.

We do not assume that every time a man gets wealthy in public office that he must have taken influence money or sold his support to the highest bidder, even though men have a high incidence of unethical behavior in political circles. Why do we have to believe that this woman, who has come this far, cheated and lied to do so? Perhaps many of us believe it because FOX news says it every day, makes little movies about it, propaganda films that are much more ads than they are news. All I can say to the Hillary haters is "stop watching FOX News."

So, after apologizing to everyone who might be offended in advance, I will do my little end zone dance – not the one that signals we have won the whole game yet, just the one that acknowledges a touchdown, a milestone for women (and men) in United States history. This is a happy moment, and it is one for the history books, so take a minute to acknowledge its importance and give Hillary and History a high five.

"YAY! HUZZAH! BRAVO! (OK, I'm done for now.)

Implications of Orlando and Beyond
June 14, 2016

For a while I loved reading anthropological fiction based on information gleaned from artefacts but peopled with made-up characters – an entire fleshed out primitive culture based only on tools, pottery shards, bones, cave drawings, and other evidence uncovered at sites where ancient people once lived. Jean Auel was one of my favorite authors in this genre. She wrote **Clan of the Cave Bear** and all the sequels that followed. Kathleen O'Neal Gear was another favorite, writing about early "tribes" of people on the American continent.

The caves where early man lived, and the long houses, offered little privacy, although there was also comfort in proximity. Family groups, separated by their fires had no wall between one family and the next. One author suggested that there was a kind of unwritten rule to "mind your own campfire." I am sure that this rule was sometimes ignored and that even the earliest people liked to "gossip." But there were social repercussions for serious disregard of familial privacy.

I will come back to this.

On another thread, our government is designed the way it is because our forefathers came from England and Western Europe where government leaders and church leaders engaged in a constant series of struggles to determine which group should have the most power. For many years the church was firmly in charge. But strong monarchs who felt they held their thrones by "divine right" did not worry so much about challenging the Pope. The impact of the seesaw squabbles between powerful forces hit the subjects/citizens hard.

In England alone, one day people were safe as Catholics, but the next monarch was a Protestant and hunted down Catholics. Eventually both of these religions were discarded, and the Anglican Church was formed, leaving both Catholics and Protestants in jeopardy. Today England has made a successful marriage of church and state, but when the colonists came to America that was not the case either in England or on the continent, and so our forefathers legislated the separation of church and state, and freedom of religion.

Except in Spain the Muslim religion was not an issue as America was being born but I still don't believe our forefathers would say that only Christians should be free to worship as they please. It does seem clear to most of us that our forebears would not require the Federal government of the United States of America to follow the dictates of any particular religion.

Republicans, who hate that women are free to make their own choices about whether to end a pregnancy or carry a fetus to term, want to make us believe that our forefathers did not actually separate church and state, that they were all Christians, and that the freedom they wrote into our founding documents referred only to Christians. Republicans want to deny the separation of church and state because their case against Roe v Wade is argued on grounds of Christian morality which is at odds with such a separation. In other words, they want to impose a Fundamentalist interpretation of religion on all of us.

The Republicans also want to exclude all Muslims from immigrating to America because they see possible clashes between Christians and Muslims in America. Lately it seems as if the Crusades were simply put on hold and are now in danger of being resurrected. But the freedom of religion our forefathers laid down in our founding documents is not a qualified freedom, it applies to all. In addition to the rights of women we now have Americans who are unhappy that human rights have been extended to same-sex couples. Many Christians believe God would not like this – it is against the Bible – it is an abomination – it is Sodom and Gomorrah. These folks carry hate and anger in their hearts and fear of their God.

Apparently, the Muslim religion finds same-sex relationships unnatural also and they are equally anathema, a sign of a decadent culture that is off the rails and therefore a target – rich situation for a militant "hero" (terrorist) who plans to be rewarded in "the next life." I suppose some American Christians might be horrified if they could really see the connections they have on this issue with radical Muslims. Although the GOP inveighs against Sharia law, the moral judgments of the two groups are very similar.

So here we have this social group – gay people, LGBT+ - or any other identifier -that is a focus of hatred for at least two groups of Fundamentalists that are committing vigilante acts in a country that believes that there is a firm separation between the secular and the religious. They are operating outside the laws of the nation, but they believe they are operating within a higher law, the law of their God. (Christian Pro Life groups have murdered abortion providers and have vilified same-sex relationships and radical Muslims might kill almost any Christian, but also use same-sex relationships to focus their religious rage.)

I guess we are at a moment when it will be decided whether our societies will be ruled by God (through men) or by man. Either way we are still dealing with man's interpretations of religious laws written tens of centuries ago and document written several centuries ago. Except that today we have a global population of billions and complex cultures that have resulted from organizing so many humans, so trying to follow laws made for sparsely populated, somewhat nomadic desert cultures presents many anomalies, not least of which is who gets to decide what is the appropriate literal interpretation of those ancient laws.

How will we resolve this dilemma – this war of ideals between citizens who believe in the separation of church and state and the human rights of all, and citizens who feel that the government is treading on the turf of religion? Granting human rights to folks whose sexual orientation is often genetically coded into their DNA seems appropriate. In fact, a culture that celebrates freedom, ensuring the human rights of all who are not criminals should be desirable. However, for some, granting human rights to some folks turns those that have a religious objection not only into losers, but also into sinners.

So, this whole train of thought brings us back to our very earliest forbears and their unwritten rule to "mind your own campfire." It is certainly overly simplistic but if people only made it their mantra, we might take scary hot-button trends that are escalating and calm them down, defuse them, so that our new refrain could be more "live and let live" and less of a personal/sacred affront that must be avenged to insure an afterlife in whatever heaven one subscribes to. These days we say, "mind your own business" and it would be great if people practiced this whenever possible, meaning whenever life or safety is not an issue.

Because our Congress refuses to act, this is the best idea I have after the terrible events in Orlando this weekend, and isn't much against bullets, hate, and fear. But the larger implications of Orlando and beyond tell us that until it is decided just how much religion we want in our government and how may guns it will take to satisfy the Second Amendment, it may be best to stay as simple as possible.

2016 Election: Should One Party Control All Three Branches of Government?
June 24, 2016

If we elect a Republican President, we will, for the first time ever give Republicans control of all three branches of government. I might start an argument with this statement, but I can offer justification for it. In the past the Supreme Court has not been counted when determining the balance of power in Washington because the Supreme Court has been held to be nonpartisan. However, if you have been paying attention to politics recently, Republicans and Democrats each give being able to fill the current and near-term empty seats on the Court with nominees generated by their particular party as a deciding factor in who we should elect.

The Republicans tell their people that appointments to the Supreme Court are the most important reason to elect a Republican President, even if it is Donald Trump. We already have Donald's list of eleven people that Republican might like to appoint to the Court during their tenure. Does this sound nonpartisan to you? And of course, the Democrats would also like to make the next court appointments. In fact, there is a vacancy right now and we do have a Democrat for a President. Obama has played nice and picked a moderate appointee, but Republicans will not give this respected figure consideration.

I do not believe that we can count the Supreme Court or even the Federal Courts as being nonpartisan any longer and this puts justice up for grabs. Whose brand of justice shall we have? The courts are not big prizes for "we the people" in elections because we don't elect most judges. They are appointed by the President and approved by Congress. They are usually appointed for life which makes the courts a prize that keeps on giving even after your party has left office. Right now the Federal Courts are overwhelmingly in the hands of Conservative appointees, and there are many vacancies which should have been filled by President Obama, and might have been filled given a more moderate Republican Party. This incarnation of the Republican Party, extreme and very right wing, in take-no-prisoners mode, has left many benches empty rather than allow Obama's appointments to be seated. In this way the GOP turns the courts into a bipartisan branch of our government, and they are holding the courts hostage until we elect a Republican President or until they lose their majority.

It is somewhat common for one party to control the Executive and Legislative branches of government, but it is difficult to get any information about control of the Supreme Court because the myth remains that it is a nonpartisan body even when everyday evidence suggests that it is not so. Yesterday was a perfect example because the number of justices, usually 9, is down to 8 Supremes, so the Court is giving us a string of 4-4 tied decisions on a number of what could have been landmark cases. The fact that there can be a tie proves that the court is bipartisan and, while John Roberts was crossing party lines according to his reading of the law and his conscience, he is less likely to put himself in such a position right now, although he might do so if the case were so important that not deciding it would destroy America. Let's hope we don't have to test that out.

I am just trying to make sure that we are all very clear
about the ramifications of electing any Republican as
our President in 2016, whether it is Mr. Trump or
not. If you do this thing (because I will not), unless at
least one House of Congress changes its majority
party, you will give Republicans carte blanche to enact
their entire program which will include things like
closing the Department of Education, closing the
Department of Commerce, and perhaps a few others
to drastically downsize government.

The GOP may not immediately make Social Security a
voucher program, but they will pare our social safety
net to the bone and whether you are poor or not, it
will affect your life. They will bust our labor unions,
and they will deregulate Wall Street, banking and
investing, and you will let them because they will tell
you that it will bring jobs back (which I very much
doubt). They will cut taxes on the wealthiest
Americans. They will change our health care system
by repealing the Affordable Care Act and I am betting
we will lose coverage for pre-existing conditions. And
if Donald gets his way, they will build a wall, leave
NATO, and round up illegal immigrants for
expulsion. This list is long, and you can hear them
extol it every day. And they will pack those courts
with so many Conservatives that no woman in
America will ever be able to choose whether she
wants to start a family or have another child for

decades, and we will be finding a lot more religion mixed into our governance.

So, I am asking Americans to exercise some restraint and common sense and to not let all three branches of our government fall under the control of one party. There will be no checks; there will be no balances. The GOP will just have their way with us, and it will be the end our grand experiment in Democracy.

(Today, 6/24/2016, the UK decided to Brexit the EU, a decision whose impetus came from emotions very similar to those felt by the American Trump faction. We will have until November to see how such nationalism works for Great Britain. Will humanistic isolation serve them well? Should everyone retire to their separate corners? Does the world need a time out? November is probably too close to give us a true picture of the effects of this stunning move by the people of Great Britain, but we might get some clues. And if we decide to go with the GOP in the 2016 election it comes with lots of other baggage besides nationalism, which takes us back to the question of whether we want one party in control of all three branches of our government.)

The Benghazi Report
June 28, 2016

Obviously, I am writing this and I have not read the 800 pages in the Benghazi Report. I will wait for the summary assigned to some poor intern who will have to read the whole thing, or perhaps it will be split up and shared out among interns. But I have a few things to say and luckily, because of free speech, I can say them. Besides the fact that Trey Gowdy always looks about twelve, I have to say, for the record, that despite his boyish appearance, I do not trust him. He is the king of innuendo. Innuendo is a technique to make someone feel guilty when there is not enough evidence to prove that they are. I believe he made his conclusions before the committee was ever convened and that he engineered what went on in the committee to give credence to his interpretation of events. I watched him interview witnesses and he did not let them speak. It was not conducted as an investigation, but as a tribunal.

Trey Gowdy says that this report is not about one person, and he is probably telling the truth. This is about elections – the one in 2012 and the one in 2016. Republicans are rabid to win the Presidency, and they have proven it by their strategies in the states and in Congress. The GOP believes that if the Obama administration had stressed that this was a terrorist attack happening on 9/11 then the GOP would have won the 2012 election. If they can prove that the Democrats in office deliberately dithered about their response to the Benghazi attacks because their actions would hurt them in the imminent election, and that our American guys died for reasons of political expediency, it will so disgust Americans that they will have to turn against the Democratic Party and vote for the Republican candidate even if it is Donald Trump. He uses the buck stops with her argument to convict Hillary.

Historically, diplomats have been killed during several different administrations. I have looked it up before. It is in the record. It is still unclear, after listening to the discussion on the news this morning, if a rescue force could have reached Benghazi. The chatter still says that it was impossible. Trey Gowdy asks why we didn't have troops in the area, as if Libya were the only trouble spot in these chaotic times.

These terrorist attacks apparently happened fast, they were very effective, and they were secret. This certainly has implications for our lack of intelligence, which we have discussed often enough, and which still seems to require attention, our progress more like two steps forward, one step back. It is sad if all that dithering really happened with our troops changing in and out of uniforms four times as reported. If the plane could still have not reached Benghazi on time anyway then at least the dithering did not affect the outcome and is included in the report as a rebuke on guess who.

One could propose a counter theory (of the conspiracy variety) that this attack seems to have happened at a key moment and that perhaps the GOP, so desperate to hold all the power in Washington, may have ordered this stealth attack so they would win the election – and it would have had just as much basis in fact. Impugning someone's character in this case cost the American people $7 million for a skewed committee to try to find out what was going on in the black box of Democratic minds during Benghazi. But our brains are not like the black boxes on airplanes. We don't yet know how to access the contents.

It is still sad and always will be sad to think of these American citizens in a foreign land facing such unequal odds. It is horrific to remember that they died repeatedly in the awareness that they would die and that they were not soldiers in a war but were in that country to promote peace and fairness and freedom. America will always mourn those dedicated men.

July

Shooting Black Folks Must Stop
July 6, 2016

How will we solve this problems that our nation is having with our police shooting black folks who are either guilty of nothing or of committing a petty criminal act? The list grows and grows. Trayvon Martin, Eric Garner, Michael Brown, Tamir Rice, Freddie Gray, Alton Sterling and many, many more. It looks like the police are on a secret campaign to rid themselves of black people. It looks intentional. There is a certain consistent order of events. Someone defies authority in some small way and this defiance is used as an excuse to escalate, to get the man or woman who dares to fight back verbally or act defensively to look guilty of something. Then someone off camera shouts "he's got a gun" (not usual when women are being apprehended). Then the shots ring out and there is no need for a trial or imprisonment or any official routine because the person is dead. Surprisingly the body cameras which these officers wear are often off or aimed in the wrong direction when events reach their terrible denouement.

I understand that law enforcement becomes more and more complicated as the inequalities in our culture are exposed to the light of day. I know that there are those in our communities who have committed criminal acts to get ahead when traditional pathways were closed to them. I get it that there are some mean folks out there who would as soon kill a policeman as any other human being who they felt was threatening them. I suppose that mistakes will be made. However, when the "mistakes" seem to occur frequently and when they seem to follow a certain pattern, then some action plan is called for to make it stop.

If black people are not being targeted, we must at least face the bad, bad optics of these now-all-too-familiar shootings with their attendant grief and loss. There are echoes that go back to slavery with people hunting down their runaway slaves. We must stop doing this. We must find some new ways to help our policemen and women fight crime in our communities without executing people who seem to hardly qualify as the most dangerous people on our streets. I believe that if we can't find a way out of this brutal and unjust law enforcement behavior that peaceful demonstrations will eventually turn into angry outcries. We know that the police involved will be investigated and we know how the investigation will end. If we find our police guilty in these cases, we undermine their authority.

This relatively new pattern of picking off people one-by-one is exacerbated by our guns everywhere policies enforced by the gun industry and the NRA and a Conservative interpretation of the Second Amendment. The complications and division present in our culture at this moment will make it difficult to resolve this issue. Anger is the emotion that seems to be driving current events. It doesn't matter because these shootings and the fact that they seem to fall all too often on Americans of color is a stain on our nation that could eventually destroy the freedom that is the pillar of our Democracy.

The work must be done in our communities and what we must provide young Americans of African Descent and poor Americans are pathways to a better future so that they will not be forced into antisocial behaviors by circumstances that make their lives difficult and seemingly without value. We don't need to talk any longer about doing this. We do need to talk to plan what we will do. Then we need to put our money where our mouths are and carry out our plans. Our plans will not be perfect. It is the very nature of humans that we cannot be perfect. We can't allow ourselves to be so nervous about possible negative effects that will appear down the line. We must earnestly try to solve the inequalities in our America or America will fail.

Donald Trump is Deranged
July 18, 2016

Donald Trump is deranged. It is covered over right now with engineered speeches, teleprompter puppeteering, suave political management, and a boring running mate, but the crazy is still in there. We already got to listen to it for an entire primary season. The Republican National Committee now has Donald

Trump tied down like Gulliver in Lilliput (Jonathan Swift). Donald Trump will either break free at some point and invite us to his rave once again, or his children will be running our government with the able (that's sarcasm) help of another intolerant throwback to the 50's, Mike Pence, his VP.

How did he, Donald Trump, get this far? I blame all the media, currently busy denying they had any part in this. And even more, I blame their bosses who, I am sure, insisted they televise every move Trump made in the primaries because the ratings were through the roof (today's version of events the Roman Coliseum was designed for). We know this happened because the print media and the broadcast media have both kept us informed about the money Donald didn't have to spend. Commentators on every network get to relax and let Donald script their shows for them in his shockingly unscripted way.

What does it matter now who is to blame? We are apparently stuck with this nightmare scenario. However, it does still matter. The media, even the liberal-leaning media, likes to paint Donald Trump and Hillary Clinton as being somehow equally awful. Sometimes Hillary even has a slight edge over Donald. I don't know what your favorite channel of choice is, but mine is MSNBC. At least once in almost every hour of every day someone on Morning Joe, and Meet the Press Daily, and Andrea Mitchell's show, or even the new Bloomberg offering goes on and on about Hillary's unfavorable and untrustworthy ratings and sums up *ad infinitum*, the (unproven) sins she committed that have earned her the low ratings. I have never seen anyone so maligned for so little. Even Donald Trump is not so consistently assigned to the suddenly proverbial burning dumpster, and he has done and said some truly reprehensible things.

So, although it seems clear to rational folks that Donald Trump should never be the President of the United States of America here we are watching a weeklong pretense in the form of the Republican Convention that seems to say that what we are witnessing is a normal and traditional election, when we could actually be witnessing the end of America as we know it. The entire charade is shameful and without the endless media circus might never have happened. Do your job, media people, and make sure that you find a way to repair the damage you have done before it is too late, if it isn't already.

Donald Trump is Deranged: The Details
July 21, 2016

Excerpt from: Diagnostic and Statistical Manual (IV) Criteria for Narcissistic Personality Disorder 1.
 Has a grandiose sense of self-importance.
2. Is preoccupied with fantasies of unlimited success, power, brilliance beauty, or ideal love.

3. Believes that he or she is "special" and unique and can only be understood by, or should associate with, other special or high status people (or institutions).
4. Requires excessive admiration.
5. Has a sense of entitlement.
6. Is interpersonally exploitative
7. Lacks empathy; is unwilling to recognize or identify with the feelings and needs of others.
8. Is often envious of other or believes that others are envious of him or her.
9. Shows arrogant, haughty [rude and abusive] behaviors or attitudes

Once again, I argue that Donald Trump is deranged. His derangement takes several forms. He is, first, a certifiable megalomaniac (see narcissistic personality disorder). People with this disorder are sometimes leaders because their ego drives them to destroy all obstacles in their path, but they are usually too selfish to share power with anyone. While Julius Caesar began his governance of Rome by heading a republican form of government, he soon became disillusioned with the Roman senators, and he felt that he towered over them in every way. He became "dictator in perpetuity" and the Fall of Rome began. (By the way, he was also assassinated.) Donald Trump is such a man. He does not have equals, only underlings.

He is not the right person to head a Democracy. He does not even believe in free speech unless it praises him. This should be frightening to all who love America and what we stand for. If he gets elected, I will be scared to speak against him. Is he just a verbal bully, or is he a true thug who will use power as a weapon? We don't know, do we? I was only ever nervous about speaking out against two other Presidents – Nixon and GW Bush (because of his henchmen) – both Republicans.

The Republican Party seems to think that to keep order in America we must flirt with fascism. (Donald Trump acts like a fascist.) They don't like people who speak softly even if they do carry a big stick. They want to be sure the world knows that any leader they back will talk tough and use that big stick, with malice, at the slightest offense. The problem with this is that our biggest stick is a nuke, which Donald Trump refuses to say he will only use under dire circumstances.

Donald Trump is a deal maker, which in his case means that he will do almost any sleazy old thing as long as it marginally legal. So, he tells Americans, who think our government is taking care of so many undeserving people that it can no longer take care of them, that he will build a wall – that he will kick out all the freeloaders. And he will bring back all the jobs. But if he can't do these deals, he will not mind disappointing his followers and he will do different deals which they may or may not like. That is the true "Art of the Deal."

Trump seems to have the emotional maturity of a child. Name-calling, cheap taunts, foolish nicknames, these things may look like they send opponents scurrying, but his targets only disengage because if they fight back they have to lose any gravitas they might ever have in the future. Donald is a junk yard dog who will keep throwing dirtier dirt until his temper tantrum gets him what he wants. He may seem to win but he really just sets his "phaser" to stun and those he vanquishes decide to walk away and live to fight another day.

I understand that the things he promises look appealing to some. He seems like he can bring back simpler times when Americans were predominantly Christians of European origin who spoke English. His followers seem to yearn for this and believe that he will basically give them back the America of their childhoods. The world has moved on however, and it will most likely prove impossible for Donald Trump to produce an American future that corresponds with his fantastical promises. The 21 st century is what it is and that is what we must learn to participate in, and we must prove that we know how to thrive even as our world changes. As for Donald, if he is President, I hope he gets good meds. If he is not elected, he can be as eccentric as he pleases. He is wealthy enough to get away with it.

The Last Great Conspiracy Theory?
July 24, 2016

Have we reached the last great conspiracy theory? We have been watching a conspiracy theory tennis tournament play out between the Democrats and the Republicans at least since 2012.

The Benghazi tennis ball has been smashed back and forth for ages because the damning revelations were supposed to be timed to interfere with the 2016 election. Finally, the anticlimactic report of the last Benghazi investigation (we hope it is the last because it's costing the American people big bucks) concludes that all evidence suggests that Hillary Clinton was not guilty of any wrongdoing in this devastating attack in Libya. There was no assistance that could have arrived in time to save our people in Benghazi and Hillary Clinton was not, as many state, asleep at the most crucial moments.

The fact that Hillary Clinton used a private server while at the State Department was the one juicy piece of info that came out of the Benghazi investigations. The Republicans put the Benghazi investigation to rest because they gleefully imagined that Hillary would be indicted by the FBI for something, treason, I guess. This seems a rather hyperbolic outcome to wish for given that it would suggest that Hillary is a seer who knew that the attacks in Benghazi would happen when she became Secretary of State and planned in advance to cover her tracks. But it sort of fits the Lucifer label that Republicans tried to attach to her at the RNC last week. (Republicans have a thing about Lucifer – they are so paranoid about the UN that they speak of something called the Luciferian Church of the UN, *which does not exist.*) I suspect they are saying that as Hillary is Lucifer on earth, she could have known about the Benghazi attacks in advance. If you must use this kind of bizarre reasoning to get where you want to go wouldn't it seem that it is time to backtrack and start over, or just be quiet?

So now the GOP is left with just one tennis ball to bat around and they must try to make the volleys last until Hillary is tarred and feathered just before people go to the polls because Republicans cannot win this election without sliming their opponent, considering the caliber of their own candidate. This final round of our conspiracy tournament involves the Clinton Foundation, and the arms deals made by the State Department while Hillary Clinton was Secretary of State. It is possible that these are two separate spheres that simply look like they overlap (a simple conflict of interest), or it is possible that there was collusion between Bill and Hillary and that her arms deals while in the State Department were tied to the donations made to the Clinton Foundations. I have spoken of the difficulty with seeing simple cause-effect relationships in complex matters. You must carefully connect the dots to prove that the money given to the Clinton Foundation was indeed used to influence arms deals in the State Department. The optics are bad, but is there actually any connection?

I don't recall a time when we have had a husband-and-wife team where each partner has aspirations for the Presidency of the United States of America. Had the times been different for women would Eleanor Roosevelt have made a great Presidential candidate? Possibly. But that moment didn't happen. We are fifty years past those days. We now have a past President, Bill Clinton, doing his post-Presidential best to help save the people on the planet from poverty and exploitation. And we have Hillary Clinton who believes she can do a good job as our first female President. I assume, Bill Clinton's goals are altruistic. Others assume he is using the Clinton Foundation to increase his personal wealth and bankroll his wife's election campaign. People who hypothesize about this know that such activities are illegal, and yet they believe that Bill and Hillary Clinton are so powerfully connected and privileged that they will not only steal from a charitable foundation with the family name right on it, but also that their guilt will be covered up by powerful people. That all sounds diabolical.

But is it true?

Furthermore, the argument goes on to say that Hillary drummed up contributions for the family charity while she made her rounds as Secretary of State and that she traded State Department arms deals for those contribution. There are charts hanging out on the internet that look damning. See: https://www.ibtimes.com/clinton-foundationdonors-got-weapons-deals-hillary-clintons-statedepartment-1934187

One chart is entitled 'Defense Contractors Donated to the Clinton Foundation' and another bears the caption 'Clinton Foundation Donors Get Big Weapons Deals'. There is plenty of overlap.

Looking at these two charts, I can see why people get all exercised over this. But just because events are contiguous does not prove a cause-effect relationship. If there is a true cause-effect connection between these two sets of data, then perhaps Bill and Hillary should be in jail. But even though Hillary's judgment was called into question on the email server decision, it would take some pretty stunningly unrealistic rationalizations for the Clintons to sell arms through the State Department in exchange for campaign contributions from foreign governments and make those funds look like charitable donations. Why would anyone expect to get away with something so blatantly illegal when contemplating a run for the highest office in our nation? I still do not accept that the Clintons are corrupt enough to plan and execute a scheme like this. I believe that the Clinton Foundation is Bill's project and does have charitable goals. I also believe that Hillary did not go around the globe trading ostensibly charitable contributions from foreign governments for arms offered to foreign nations by the State Department. Connect the dots if you can. If you can't retire the ball and get off the court and end this third round of the great conspiracy tennis tournament.

August

The Republican Scandal Extravaganza
August 24, 2016

So here we are, right in the direct path of the Republican scandal extravaganza, which we have known was coming. They were just waiting until fall, but they couldn't quite wait because when the FBI released that last batch of approximately 15,000 emails it was a sign. This is it! They signaled the Trump campaign, which just in a nick of time is headed by the formidable Kellyanne Conway. Let's make this an all-out effort to fatally damage Hillary Clinton, they telegraphed. And the Republicans have plenty of help with all the members of the press piling on too. There are plenty of ratings to be made folks. There has to be something really damning in those emails. There just has to be. That charity cannot just exist for humanitarian reasons. The Clintons are too greedy for that. Let's impeach those humanitarian emailers before they even get into the White House this time.

The press is in a frenzy. The AP got in on the act. They checked Hillary's State Department calendar, and she had meetings with lots of people who gave to the Clinton Foundation. Never mind that there are only so many nations on the planet and that almost all of them meet from time to time with the State Department. We smell nefarious favors being doled out by the millions. The Clinton Foundation takes money from nations with terrible records on human rights. OMG! Who needs to salve their conscience more than an authoritarian nation, and who doesn't like to have help with their nation's poorest citizens? If a nation will not contribute doesn't that brand them as villainous?

How does a skeevy guy like Donald Trump get to pass judgment, with the whole power of a major political party behind him, on anyone? Here is someone who we know scammed others for profits which lined his own pockets. Now he gets to go on TV and act holier-than-thou? That's just wrong. And if the Republican Party and Donald Trump (under the watchful eye of Ms. Conway) manage to tarnish Hillary beyond electability only Donald Trump will be left, assuming we are still not ready to elect someone from the Libertarian Party or the Green Party. The Republicans are great strategists and have planned this well and timed it right to do maximum damage very close to the November election. Doesn't it bother anyone that it reeks of mudslinging politics? I do not buy that the Clinton Foundation did anything illegal. I trust, and I am using that word deliberately, that they were busy setting up programs that helped people around the world lift themselves up and feel pride in their accomplishments.

"In the Day" and Now/Black Power
August 27, 2016

When I was just beginning my career as a teacher, I was hired to work in a program that was designed to provide equal opportunity to the poor and minorities. The program in New York State was called SEEK (Search for Education, Elevation, and Knowledge). Later the name of the program outside New York City was changed to EOC (Educational Opportunity Center). It was intended to serve as a sort of prep school in New York State's city centers, similar to the Educational Opportunity Programs on SUNY campuses; a program to boost academic levels of poor and minority adults who had left school before graduation or who had been undereducated in inner city schools that tended to educate students to an eighth-grade level (or less) and then lose them. The SEEK program began in 1965 and was a direct result of the Civil Rights Movement in America and the Civil Rights Act of 1964 and of what were relatively few violent demonstrations in some densely populated African American communities where citizens were emboldened by recent events such as the Black Power movement to demand a share of the American Dream.

So, I began teaching as a very young person with my little BA degree in Secondary English in the SEEK program and I was hired by a tall white bearded hippie to be part of this sort of harem of young (white) women who he hired to assist him in what was basically, at that time, a speed-reading program. Every student had a little speed-reading machine and a paperback novel. We, the sort of TA's, would test each student to determine their initial reading speed and we would stand in a line in the classroom and peel off as needed to assist students who were ready to adjust their speed upward. It was absurd, but I really needed a job. It went against everything I had learned about good teaching and was miles away from being a good college prep reading course, but it did give me time and perspective to think about what I would do differently when I became the department chair, which I eventually did.

For the first time in my life, at the very beginning of my career, I found myself in an environment where I, as a white person, was in the minority. The SEEK program administrator was a graduate of the University of Michigan, a powerfully energetic black man (at the time it was the choice of African Americans to be called "black") who had pulled along with him into our small provincial city the cream of the crop of his young black buddies, also from the University of Michigan. These men were educated, handsome, and very, very comfortable with each other. They were in their element. This is what they trained for and it was obvious that they wouldn't be here long. These were guys (we called them "brothers") who could be very funny. They could switch back and forth from professional language to street within a single sentence. They were very smart, and they were on their way to much bigger careers. By 1971 most of these young "Turks" had moved on.

It was intoxicating, as a young white woman, to share time in this energetic and testosterone-enhanced world with these young men who were the first and most entitled generation of African American men to benefit from the whole sad and heroic Civil Rights Movement in which many of them had taken part. I could have fallen in love with any one of them with their giant afros and wonderful smiles, but that was not what we were all about, and they had plans to marry educated sisters and live well. What we were was colleagues and we were establishing an alternative program which could funnel the poor and minorities up from the projects and into the middle class. I have carried the surprisingly vivid memories of those halcyon days with me during all my life. And, happily, although these young ambitious men did eventually leave our program and move up in the world, we were able to put together excellent preparatory courses and to send hundreds of people to college who would probably not have continued their education at all. We were able to give them the skills they needed to do well in their college studies and this, in turn, built their confidence in their ability to succeed.

It is no longer the sixties, but recent events have made it clear that we are still working out our national shortcomings in the Civil Rights arena. When George Zimmerman shot and killed Trayvon Martin, an African American teenager taking an evening walk with his cell phone to a convenient store, the wounds that remain on the American psyche reopened and we were taken back to the sixties again. In fact there was a direct connection, it was the 50 th anniversary of a day when Representative John Lewis from Georgia had been the Chairman of SNCC and one of the "Big Six" leaders of the Civil Rights movement. He helped plan the March on Washington in August of 1963 which was the occasion of MLK's "I Have a Dream" speech. Fifty years later here John Lewis is on national television reacting to the verdict in the

George Zimmerman trial and sadly confronting the fact that the work of winning equality for African Americans is not done.

In fact, television that week, after that hotly contested verdict, was chock full of more African American men and women, with their intelligent, cogent, and very professional discussions of the emotions being experienced by African Americans and the historical context for these feeling. They were able to contain what was probably some significant anger and discuss the ramifications of the trial decision, and to explain to the rest of America their problem with "Stand Your Ground" laws and the acquittal of George Zimmerman. When John Lewis spoke out, we were reminded of the cosmic irony that this trial occurred on the anniversary of the Martin Luther King speech that almost every America knows by heart. The IRS hearings brought that wonderful Elijah Cummings of Maryland to my attention with his commonsense ability to bring the soaring fiction of Darryl Issa back to earth. And I also have to mention The Grio in this mix because I was watching MSNBC much of the time and they have hired Joy-Ann Reid as an adjunct to their staff. She has great connections in the African American community, and she expresses herself clearly and powerfully. She is a real asset, as is her colleague Melissa Harris-Perry who has her own show on MSNBC. What can beat two intelligent women who also happen to be African American who can offer their sophisticated perceptions on politics in these wacky political times we are living through since 2008.

So, for a moment I was back in those faculty/staff meetings at the old SEEK program with those glowing African American men, just ready to step off into their very distinguished futures. It was good to see all those intelligent, highly educated black people who may have benefited from the programs that were developed in the 60's to diversify the American middle class. It felt a bit like old home week. Too bad it took one alleged scandal and one very sad event to hear from all those erudite black voices. Hopefully they will be consulted over other issues as we have seen on a few of the Sunday shoes.

This is a view from the cheap seats. This article first appeared on my website on 8/7/2013.

The Bully vs. the Wonk: The Presidential Debates August 29, 2016

On September 26 th Hillary Clinton and Donald Trump will appear in the first debate that puts these two in the same venue on a stage together. There will be some rules and there will be moderators, but I still think that this is a terrible idea. I am usually all in favor of debates. But I dread this one. I picture it as the bully vs. the wonk. It's not that Hillary can't handle herself in just about any situation. If you want to be the President of the United States of America, you cannot back down from confrontation. And right now, the toughest tickets are not people in foreign governments or countries. Foreign leaders try to be polite in their dealings even when they are saying no. These days some of meanest suits are on people right here in our own country. Hillary is not afraid of these people. She thinks she can even win some of them over to consider compromises that will move our nation forward, and we wish she could do that, although most of us think she is in for the same realities that Obama has faced.

Hillary has taken stands on the issues that are important to Americans in 2016, and she would welcome a chance to stand up and make her points in a public way in front of all of America. But she is unlikely to get to do any such thing. She is more likely to be the focus of Donald Trump's degrading attentions and to be beaten over the head by his propaganda cudgels such as name-calling, lying smears, and patently untrue nonsense, linguistic tricks that nevertheless all have ways of leaving marks on his opponents. How many times will he call her "lyin' Hillary" and bring up the totally bogus "racist" label he has decided to graffiti on her this time? How many times will he bring up the Clinton Foundation and the "pay to play" that never happened? Donald Trump has no filter. Apparently, truth has fled the political arena for good.

Except that when Hillary discusses the issues, she wants to pursue I feel that she is being honest about what she would like to do, that she has spent time and energy designing approaches to these issues. She wants to target the poor and the middle class and stop skewing our economy towards those who are already wealthy. Donald has given us little of substance on the issues except to assure us that whatever little or big thing it is that bothers us, he will fix it (bigly). It is difficult to know what Hillary intends to do to tackle issues in foreign affairs because she has not said what she will do in Afghanistan or Iraq. She has mentioned a few plans such as a no-fly zone to deal with the black hole of sadness, grief, and outrage that defines Assad's refusal to release Syria from his clutches. Donald, however, has offered to cut loose our allies in NATO and either nuke our enemies or give them nukes so they can erase each other from the face of the earth (along with untold numbers of us).

If they could both be held to discussions of policy only, no slurs allowed, then this debate might be a real eye-opener for America. Then instead of the bully vs. the wonk; it might be wonk v wonk. However, I am fairly certain that the debate will just devolve into watching the first female candidate with a chance to win a Presidential election bashed continuously, without much of a chance to respond, by a man who has already proven himself to be unfit for the office of the Presidency, in front of a cheering crowd looking for the death blow - thus proving that those Mad Max movies were right. We are the exact same primitive humans who relished watching mayhem at the Roman Coliseum many centuries ago. I will be more than happy to skip this debate which the media is so looking forward to. I think I will avoid the bloodletting. Perhaps I will wait and catch the clips and commentaries that are sur to follow.

The Red Line – Syria Then and Now
August 30, 2016

What I said then:

What is it with men? Do women draw "red lines"? I have never heard a woman draw such a line, a line in the sand, a line on the playground, a line which everyone understands means "cross this line and there will be consequences," physical consequences, unpleasant consequences (well maybe women do that with their offspring and their partners). Netanyahu drew a red line about nukes and Iran. This red line has not been crossed yet, but Israel lives "in the hood" and is lobbing bombs at neighboring aggressors. It's only a matter of time. Obama also drew a red line that implied America would punish Assad in Syria if he used chemical weapons against his own people. Is this a testosterone thing? But in the case of Assad, a totalitarian monster who will fight in the face of millions of refugees (his own people), and who will make them flee their own country; a little thing like a "red line" won't stop a man like this. It acts like a red cape acts on a bull. But the red line has been drawn, a gauntlet has been laid down, and Assad has challenged Obama to a duel. Dueling has been illegal for a long, long time. A red line can be redrawn. This is one option, just redraw the damn line. It doesn't matter if we look weak because we aren't weak. It shows wisdom to be able to back down from a position when someone is baiting a trap with dead children. How does a decent man beat a monster? He uses his brain, not his muscle.

What I say now:

Obama has been criticized again and again for not enforcing that red line. The Republicans have told America that the fact that we did not do something, some unknown ninja move, proves that Obama is weak, and because he is our President it makes America look weak. It invites other nations to challenge us to see how wimpy we will be. But, realistically, short of war, what were Obama's choices? Our soldiers were still traumatized by too many consecutive tours of duty in Iraq. Americans had no taste for sending our guys into Syria to fight Assad. Assad's government was and is backed by the power of Putin in Russia. Going to war with Assad could have been interpreted as an act of aggression against Russia, although I doubt that Putin wants an all-out war with America right now. Obama's deal with Putin to make sure that Assad's chemical weapons were destroyed was probably the best deal we could get at the time. Congress was busting Obama's chops for being too involved in places like Egypt and Libya. He could not have pleased the GOP no matter what he decided to do. News sources are suggesting that not all of Assad's chemical weapons were destroyed and that he may, in these late summer days of 2016 be using them again. I still like my suggestion from the days immediately after the red line was crossed.

What I said then:

If you can remember back far enough to remember the movie **Dangerous Liaisons** then I think we could find a way to register our deep, deep disapproval without lobbing bombs at a leader who is just waiting to have us lob bombs at him. (What if all hell breaks loose?) If you remember, in the movie, an aging countess (Glenn Close) had learned to use men as pawns to give to herself the independence and the power to live well without a husband. She had affairs, as many as she wanted and she manipulated guilt and the fear of exposure the men felt in such a way that when she ended the affair, they found they could not tell. She lived above gossip and although women knew she was not quite the thing, they had no proof, and she was accepted in society. Until she fell in love.

She sent that young man (John Malkovich) on his way too, but when the film begins we meet a woman who is now showing her age. She is still handsome, but not beautiful. When that young man she fell in love with comes back and implies that he is still interested, she plays her last and most dangerous game, which she loses, rather badly. She still thinks she has kept her secrets and has enough social cachet to go on. She appears at the opera, and everyone boos her, her reaction is visceral, and I'm sure that from that time forward her social isolation is complete.

Maybe we could all, in every city and town all around the world, play, over very large loudspeakers, at a certain time, like midnight at the Prime Meridian on Monday, a soundtrack of people booing with all of the loudspeakers pointed in the direction of Syria. I wonder if the sound would carry all the way to Syria. Then everyone in the world would turn his/her back on Assad and send Assad into a social isolation that would put him out of commission for the rest of his life. Now that would be retribution, and it would feel really fine. I don't imagine words, or even world-wide condemnation could affect someone as tone deaf as Assad. I don't even think bombs will do it.

What I think now:

Obviously, we are way past the days when social shunning will put even a dent in the entitled arrogant man with the heart of granite who leads Syria. Here is a man who lives in a bubble of comfort and privilege and who will not abdicate power even though his "kingdom" has been reduced to rubble around him, and his "subjects" have had to flee or die. Here is a man whose every little hair on his smarmy head is glued in place and whose wardrobe costs more than it would take to feed the starving children in the nation that is unlucky enough to be ruled by this egomaniac.

But what will finally oust this guy from his palace? Will we declare war on Assad and let the repercussions in Russia fall where they may? What if this becomes World War III and this time Russia is not on our side? I don't know anyone who really thinks that we shouldn't tread carefully, harden our hearts against letting grief and empathy dictate policy. I don't really know what Obama should do on behalf of America any more than it sounds like anyone else does, but this situation seems to call out for a creative and global strategy. People who do monstrous things often have very hard shells.

What I also think now:

If some of you think you have the perfect answer publish it so we can all see it and consider it. If, as I believe is true, no one is sure about how to handle Syria beyond what we are doing, then our choices are to continue to give Syrian refugees room to catch their breath and raise their children and to continue the air assault on Syria, the one that is further complicated by the presence of ISIS.

This is a view from the cheap seats.

This article is a reprint of an article I posted on 8/30/2013 with the title "What is it with Men?

September

Time for Single Payer Health Care
September 9, 2016

It's time for Single Payer Health Care. Obamacare has had some great moments. Many people who could never afford insurance now have it. People with preexisting conditions, once excluded from health insurance to assist them with their health expenses, now have coverage.

Obamacare has also been hard on some people in the middle class. You do not have to be in the upper middle class to be faced with these hardships. Retired couples are being faced with huge yearly fees for health care, high deductibles, and high copays.

Someone on my Facebook feed, someone who worked all her life, with a husband who worked all his life said they have to pay $6000/year and that this does not cover office visits and tests. This couple is not poor, but neither are they wealthy. Whatever they have was earned through hard work and smart financial management. So, they have a house, not a McMansion, they have a camp, not exactly a Hamptons Beach House, and they have a small boat. They have grandchildren and a dog, and they live modestly, not flamboyantly. This is just one story, but I have heard it over and over again from family and friends.

Obama dealt fairly with the insurance companies as far as I can determine. He did not go for Single Payer Insurance. He got the health insurance companies to accept some compromises, and he designed a plan that featured a private/public partnership. But insurance providers like Aetna and United Healthcare are no longer happy with the compromises they negotiated, and they are backing out of the deal. They say that their stockholders are not pleased, or their profits are too low, or even that they are losing money. If the insurance companies back out Obamacare is basically dead, it seems to me.

America accrued some important benefits from Obamacare that are not health related. Lots of people who work for private health insurance providers kept their jobs, and I do mean lots of people. If the insurance companies vacate the deal that allows Obamacare to function, then Obamacare will eventually go away and lots of Republicans will open champagne.

But there will be backlash. All of those who were once uninsured and who have had pretty good insurance for a while will not, I think, quietly accept having it snatched away. Although the insurance companies may believe they can go back to their old ways of doing business, I do not think that will fly. What other option will we have to try except a Single Payer Health Care Plan for which there is already a considerable drumbeat? People who are paying giant fees for their insurance may be quite willing to pay higher taxes to allow the federal government to back such a plan, perhaps modeled on that in England or in Canada.

There was a cartoon that once accompanied this article by Jowik. I can't print it here because I don't have permission, but I can describe it; One panel shows we the people saying, "A single payer, universal, public-funded national health plan will save millions of dollars and offer preventive medicine, individual choice of doctor, mobility, etc. - the other panel show three portly men in suits and they are labeled as Insurance companies, Drug firms, For-Profit hospitals. We listen in on them saying, "Yeah, but we would lose millions, so <u>forget</u> it. Who do you think is in charge here anyhow?

Single payer may also be the only plan that will offer enough public leverage against the pharmaceutical companies to bring down prices of the meds we use. And a single payer program will offer lots of jobs, although they might have to accept lower wages. Doctors, health professionals, and hospitals, clinics, etc., already living with the lower wages offered through Medicare will find that their wages will be lower across the board. That could make for some unhappy health care providers. Will they move to China? Probably not. Will the quality of health care go down? That is a possibility. Some single payer systems seem to involve longer wait times.

There is plenty for both the insurance providers and the insured to think about here. A for-profit health model seems unsuited to maintaining health or treating those whose health is challenged because the model is too focused on profits to do tasks that are basically humanitarian in nature at affordable rates. And yet the people who are somewhat overburdened right now in terms of paying more for health care than they should have to pay may not be willing to pay higher taxes and get less quality through a Single Payer Health Care system.

The Deplorable, the Republicans, and the Media September 13, 2016

I will eventually get to the "deplorables," but you must be patient while I make all the connections I need to make in order to make my points believable. Bear with me while I fill in the backstory. Even though it sounds overly familiar, follow along with it one more time. Recent events have their roots in the past, as is usually true with all human endeavors.

Strange Bedfellows Reprise

I once painted a word picture of a bed full of strange bedfellows with the hardworking average Americans on one side of the bed with their corporate bosses who either still employ them or who have abandoned them on the other side of the bed and as the pillow that separates these two normally adversarial groups is the Republican Party.

Nestled in with these hardworking average American are some right-wing fringe groups of Americans, the militia folks who turned out to start a war over Cliven Bundy, and yes, the haters, the misogynists, the xenophobes, the homophobes, the anti-Semites the racists, those who never accepted that the

Confederacy lost the Civil War, and even perhaps downright Fascists, and neo-Nazis. I made it seem to be mystifying that these folks were in the same bed, but it really isn't all that surprising.

Republican Media and Strange Bedfellows

The ideological glue that holds these people so unnaturally together is what the GOP has been sending out over the radio waves (the radio!) in those Talk Radio shows of Glenn Beck, Rush Limbaugh, Mark Levin, and others for more than a decade. Republicans certainly knew their audience. They did not aim for Big Business, they colluded with Big Business. Their party was dwindling in influence and size. They needed voters. So, the GOP, through their media, began saying the things that they knew would resonate with truckers on long distance trips, displaced workers tuning in at home in garages, or in their cars.

They began to say that America was being ruined, that America was being downgraded to a second-rate nation; that our leaders were knuckling under to China and at the mercy of Islamic terrorists. They took little or no responsibility for our factories relocating to the East. They took no responsibility for helping to pass laws that took away penalties, or at least did not levy penalties on companies who took their factories elsewhere where there was cheaper labor and lots of fresh consumers. They blamed the Democrats for trade deals and high taxes and too many regulations, for being in cahoots with demanding labor unions, and for environmental regulations, although many of these measures had appealed to our officials on both sides of the aisle. They seduced their listeners by speaking back to them the things that they said to each other when they gathered together. For the most part this was guy stuff, although now husbands have brought their wives along with them and many single women who lost employment have also joined the movement.

Once Fox News went on TV and said in living color, in a format that looked exactly like news (but wasn't) what the Talk Radio people had been whispering in American ears in black and white, the GOP realized that they had hit on a formula that could well put them back in the White House. When they added in the Patriot talk, the veneration of the flag, and took to the airwaves as the sole protectors of veterans America was theirs, at least the white, immigrated in or before the 19 th century, bunch.

I watched the party grow their influence and it did look like the waves of grain that symbolize the American heartland (another word they latched onto with everyone sending each other little hearts on Facebook). They hypnotized America, they brainwashed America, and they turned workers who had no work into pod people. They occupied their brains and promised them exactly what they wanted. They said they would get their jobs back and they made sure everyone could own a gun just in case they could no longer trust their government.

This is how people who did not wear suits except to weddings and funerals ended up in that bed with all the Suits.

How Republican Media called out to the Deplorables

The Republican Party has been using their own media to demonize Democrats. Media once tried to go for a balanced approach that sort of gave credence to the policies advocated by either side. The Republicans created a deliberately partisan media that spouted anti-Democrat messaging 24 hours a day. It is probably why the new idiom "24/7" was invented.

The GOP made the Democratic Party the party of immigrants so they could blame job loss on immigrants, especially immigrants who did not enter American through legal channels. They told workers who had to take jobs that paid far less than their old jobs that their tax dollars were being given to these illegal immigrants. Their tax dollars were being given to people who had never held a job or never would, and they painted those people's skin as black. That is how they fed into and strengthened an image of the freeloading "other" that already existed.

Too bad the intelligence we have about terrorists is not as good as the intelligence the Republicans have about the American middle class. Of course, the Republicans are the party that created the NSA with the Patriot Acts. When a black man became our American President that was truly serendipity. Implying that he was not a true American, that he was not a Christian, that he belonged to a church that spewed hate about white folks in America – bonanza!

Are all the white Americans who have been wooed and won by nonstop propaganda deplorable? I don't think so. Are there deplorable individuals who climbed aboard the GOP train because the rhetoric resonated with their own narrow-minded beliefs? Absolutely. Are there quite a few of them? Sadly, it seems that there might be. Do people who are not deplorable hold to some deplorable ideas? I would have to say that that is true.

Is the tribalism that defines the American social landscape deplorable? Will it lead us to anything positive if we are at each other's throats? Can you make a better future when people are so invested in their own mindset that they want to lash out at anyone who thinks differently? Will dividing America into tribes who defend their territory, separating us all

with hate and bile, eventually produce an America
that links arms and unites to produce a more peaceful
world in which we all can live? How can dividing into
separate camps ever lead to unity, tolerance, and the
creative spirit we need to meet the challenges of our
tiny planet hurtling through space.

The Republicans have exploited our differences and
exaggerated our differences to gin up votes because
they want, they desire, they must control all three
branches of government. They must truly believe that
they can restore America to a former glory that has
never really been lost. Although we may be in a down
cycle right now and recent developments abroad have
given us more competition, we are still a great nation
and a world leader.

The Republicans profess their policies in almost
biblical tones. They are trained to repeat talking
points, to talk over their opponents, to obliterate foes
with data, even if the data is made up. They must
think that "trickle-down economics" and cutting taxes
and getting rid of regulations on business and
investment, privatizing everything and building our
military while cutting the size of federal government,
that all these strategies are the Holy Grail to
reproducing the America that used to be so powerful
and so productive.

But the GOP did not trust the American people to understand how successful their policies might be because so many of us do not agree that these policies will improve America. They still had to use propaganda to win. If you have right on your side, why would you create this whole matrix of mesmerizing mind games?

Will Donald Trump and his band of Deplorables Make America Great Again?

Now the GOP is the party of Donald Trump who is the pied piper of the "deplorables," regardless of how shocked the Republicans act about what Hillary said. In the future qualities like xenophobia, racism, and misogyny will not help us create the global society, which is evolving whether we like it or not. These feelings are backward and really don't belong in a nation that espouses equality. They will only produce a more primitive America, not a futuristic America. The fact that these people have found a home in the Republican Party with Donald Trump at its helm is the best reason of all to elect Democrats in 2016. We need to fight these feelings in ourselves and not give them free rein.

October

Hillary Clinton, Up Against Misogyny, is a Fight Girl October 15, 2016

I am looking forward to our first Madam President. But there are a few things to say about the explosions of misogyny that have characterized a lot of the media coverage of the 2016 election. You would expect this to be a normal election even though it could end in a landmark historical moment, but it has been anything but normal. At this point many may put a finger (not that finger) in the air to signify "wait a minute." "I have just one point" and they would say, "if only that first woman wasn't Hillary Rodham Clinton." But it is, and despite all the cries of "fixed elections" and "rigged systems" and emails and Benghazi and the Clinton Foundation she has wended her way through our complex and overheated election process to be where she is now, and I would say that she did not use the system in any way that it has not been used by men. Even if you are one of those who argue that the system needs reform, it has not been reformed yet and she has had to understand and compete within our election process as it currently is configured, flaws and all.

Psychologists tell us we all have a fight/flight instinct. We need both because there are times to flee and times to fight. But often one impulse is stronger depending on the individual. Women have fight or flight wiring too. Hillary is a fight girl. She doesn't knuckle under, not even in her personal life. When women succumb to her husband's charms she attacks. She is a fight girl. Women understand this and applaud it in movies, in commercials, on the internet, and when Carrie Underwood sings about it. Why do they expect Hillary to hold back when her career could be on the line?

Perhaps women resent a woman so focused on success and career. But women have had enough oppression, conscious and unconscious from men; you would think other women would understand Hillary's ambitions. Do you think Hillary would be running as the first major party candidate for the Presidency of the United States if she hadn't been single-minded, and perhaps even a bit ruthless? We still expect women to be nice. We all like "nice" people. But there is some proverbial wisdom about this – "nice guys finish last"- and even though it has the word guys in it, the sentiment is generic. Whenever I get a load of her opponent, I am glad that this is a strong woman with a well-developed fight response.

I don't even know if it was by chance or by design that this first and very prepared woman candidate did not get to trade ideas with a real politician but instead had to take part in the Donald Trump side show, which was on the media day and night because no serious talk was interesting enough to compete. The media replaced women commentators with men who they believed had more gravitas and could get higher ratings, which of course they did. So, the only women we got to listen to were the "expert" journalists and campaign people who joined the round tables, and since someone like Kellyanne Conway pulled in higher ratings than any of the Clinton surrogates or supporters the female voices we heard most often were anti-Hillary. How did it happen that Republican men were able to make Hillary the key "monster" exhibited in the DT side show while the really freaky showstopper got away with being treated as nearly normal?

I heard the media people express some guilt about covering Trump events day after day. It is true that he held big rallies and Hillary tended to favor smaller and less spectacular events which did not qualify as "good TV." Still the media clearly understood that Trump was using them and saving lots of money in the process. I suppose their jobs were on the line. But while Hillary slogged it out in a real political campaign the Trump show assailed us all nonstop. Some may not see any misogyny in this, but just the fact that a ridiculous and dangerous man like DT was treated better in the media than the woman who spent her life learning how to be a political leader suggests otherwise. After the displays men have been putting on lately, I can't wait to have a woman in the White House and as many women in the Congress as we can elect. I hope it happens in 2016. After all, Hillary Clinton is a fight girl.

Sharknado Live, Death Throes of the Dominant Male October 16, 2016

The sharks are circling all around the world. Are these the final death throes of the dominant male? Have most men evolved so much that there are only a few of these critters in existence? Are they fighting against their inevitable extinction? The list is long. We have Kim Jong un in North Korea, Vladimir Putin in Russia, Bashar al-Assad in Syria, Abu Bakr al-Baghdadi with ISIS, Rodrigo Duterte in the Philippines; all sharks, all circling, all trying to preserve a style of government (male dominated dictatorship) that is becoming increasingly obsolete (and good riddance). Even in America we have Donald Trump who wants to swim with the sharks and has a few dictatorial moves of his own waiting to be implemented right here in the heart of our Democracy.

We have plenty of smaller sharks lurking close to home in the tepid waters of the America Congress, still very much dominated by men, some of them scarily un-evolved, most for some reason lurking around in the GOP. These men have made it clear that they like their women submissive or focused on the next life, waiting for the Rapture. They form all male committees to discuss issues that deeply affect the lives of women, and they do not find this the least bit unnatural or sexist.

Are the sharks so nervous at the idea of having a woman as the President of United States that they feel the need to circle closer and closer trying to unnerve the unlucky applicant for the position? How long ago did they start working on the various conspiracy theories that they have circulated to take big bites out of that first hapless female candidate? Of course, you man argue that the sharks had an easy job of it because the Clintons lived in such a target-rich environment, but at least the Clintons have tried to accomplish good things out in the world, even while they also focused on winning the 2016 election. What have the sharks in suits, who have spent the past 8 years sitting in Congress pining for power and whining at the loss of it done for you lately, or for anyone? They have obstructed, that's what they have done and it has cost Americans lots of tax dollars and, I'm thinking, a good deal of potential job growth.

Social Class and Hillary
October 18, 2016

I like to maintain a certain age anonymity, but I must confess that I lived through the same times as Hillary Clinton. We both left our families and set forth into the larger world just about 50 years before this election is taking place. I understand the sexism she had to ignore to do the things she has done. My high school guidance counselor steered me away from a career as an architect by telling me that that I was a woman, and my math was not strong enough.

Well, she was right about my math skills, and it would have been a struggle, but tutoring probably could have overcome my lack of quantitative strength. Looking back though, I can see that architecture was probably no career for a poor girl because there is a long, arduous apprenticeship before you become an actual architect and able to earn enough to pay for the education and time served in the ranks. You also have to be certain that you can build buildings that won't fall down, and it takes a strong ego to back that up. Strong egos are often hard to come by in poor families.

And I also know that, although Hillary's family was not as poor as mine, Hillary had to ignore a class system that was much more rigid than it is today. In fact, in high school, I wrote a paper about social class in America. In case you haven't noticed we still have social classes. Today on Morning Joe, Joe and Mika mentioned one of the new names used to designate the upper crust. Some rich folks are now called "coastal elites'" meaning people on the east and west coasts of America who attended elite schools and came from elite families. My family was poorer than Hillary's family. In fact, it was a real dilemma for my family that I wanted to go to any four year college at all, even a state university (we have very good state universities in New York). But Hillary's ambitions were higher than mine. My family was a lower-class blue-collar family. Hillary's father owned his own business and as such was white collar, middle class. But he was still no coastal elite.

Hillary's decision to go to Wellesley College shows a lot of moxie. She had to know that she was smart enough to apply, be accepted, and succeed. She picked a college where her own social roots would make her somewhat of an outsider. Apparently, her own parents did not even want her to go to Wellesley. Was Hillary unaware that her classmates might look down on her as an arriviste of sorts, a fish out of water, or was she totally aware of the social risks involved but felt confident that she would be accepted on her terms? Hillary continued on to Yale Law School. Is this the kind of confidence that has stayed with Hillary as she tackled positions way above the comfort level of most women from similar middle class background. She did not take refuge in the intelligentsia where many less socially confident bright women might take refuge.

What is it like for an activist from Wellesley to marry a Southern boy and go live in Little Rock? This is the stuff of novels. It is not always easy for a northern liberated girl to make herself welcome. Was she ever totally accepted there as an elite because of her Wellesley degree? Bill Clinton's mom had no easy life, and his stepfather was an abusive alcoholic so he was no elite either. He was very bright, however and he was able to get a degree from Georgetown University and was a Rhodes Scholar at Oxford in England. It is possible that he was born with that charisma which has been his ticket into elite political circles.

Hillary married Bill Clinton in 1975, and he became the Attorney General of Alabama in 1977 so it is possible that being married to a man in public office made life in a southern town easier for this woman born and raised in suburban Chicago. These two seem to have been able to enter the echelons of the upper crust or become "coastal elites" by way of the colleges they chose to attend, but it may be possible that they have never really been accepted as anything but "nouveau" interlopers.

How much does the fact that Hillary and Bill occupy social positions well above their humble origins contribute to Hillary's unfavorable ratings? Is America snobbish? Are some of us jealous? We don't seem to always like people who are born wealthy and powerful and yet we don't seems ready to accept people who made the climb up the social ladder through 'social climbing' either. Hillary seems to have climbed through academic choices and activism and people are not at all sure that the ways in which the Clintons got their money were in line with either their avowed beliefs or were accomplished by means that were totally uncorrupt. In fact, some people seem to see them as nothing short of "cons" who stole from the poor to give to themselves. Why do so many of us seem to like this version of the story although there is little proof that it is true?

So, Hillary gets the triple whammy of sexism, ageism, and classism along with a more than healthy conspiracy theory mill that spins crimes for her to be guilty of day after day. People think she should be further ahead in the polls. With all these headwinds to push against it is a wonder she is as strong as she is. It is sad that someone who has worked so hard to be of use to the nation she loves is possibly only winning because her opponent is a man who should never be the President of America. And that has everything to do with a lack of class, social or otherwise.

I do not know what kind of President Hillary Clinton will be if she is elected. If she doesn't get a left leaning Congress she will be sidelined and unable to do much more than act as a figurehead of a first female president. If she does get a Congress that leans a bit left, what will she set out to accomplish for Americans and will she be successful? But because we came up through the same cultural times in our nation and because we both experienced that reality as women, I feel we sort of had to swim in the same ocean, and I admire her because she has been a much stronger swimmer than I. I have faith that she has at least one more strong marathon swim in her.

Running Out of Time
October 22, 2016

We do not have time to legislate morality and it is not even appropriate to do so in America. We have issues of life and death to consider like how to reverse climate change on our planet if it becomes impossible to survive here. We need to decide what we will do if the air becomes un-breath-able, if the water becomes undrinkable.

We don't need to go back over things that have already been decided. We don't need to rethink birth control, or a woman's right to make decisions about her life and body including being able to have an abortion if she so chooses. Deciding exactly when life begins is irrelevant in these circumstances where the population of earth is well over 7 billion.

We need to plan for how we will feed the world's people. We need to enlist everyone's help make some tough decisions about our survival as species.

We don't have time to revisit whether the US will become a religious nation. It was already decided by our forefathers. We keep our government and our religion separate because our nation believes in freedom of religion and there are not different ways to parse this.

We do not have time for a new civil war over nonsense like whether our government will be large or small, whether it will be all white, all male or all diversified as to gender and race. Diversity is here and we don't have time to reverse it. That cannot be a priority.

We don't have time to worry about people's sexual orientation. It doesn't really matter.

We don't have time for sectarian violence and all the ideological/religious chaos around the world. It is time to pretend that aliens have attacked us, and we must unite to repel them. Of course, so far there are not any aliens, but nevertheless the planet is under attack and being destroyed. The reports about what we are doing to the earth are never good these days.

We don't have time for climate deniers and Creationists. If they have their way, we will lose the freedom we need to adopt laws that will help us meet the need of humans without destroying the home planet we are unable to leave.

We do not have time to fight about whether we should buck up the poor or let them die off if they can't take care of their own needs. Perhaps someone from those humans at the bottom of the economy may offer valuable ideas that will help us all. We cannot afford the instability that will ensue if we no longer support our poorest citizens. We need to concentrate on human survival on earth. We need to expand our space program drastically so that, if we can't save the planet, we can send some or all humans to a new planet to insure survival of the species.

We do not have time to attack our schools and make war on education. We can't un-eat that apple from Eden, reverse that original sin. Ignorance will not bring back our innocence. It can't be considered acceptable that keeping people uneducated will create a more malleable underclass. Who, except modern Republicans, thinks like that?

Maybe I've gone off the deep end and things are not nearly as dire as they seem to me, but it can't hurt to try to create a better future through conservation, better organization, cooperation, and thinking way outside the box. Perhaps there is so much distraction, escapism, and division all around the world because somewhere, at our core, we recognize that we are living in an age that represents a turning point, a pivot. We will either pivot back to a more primitive, less populated, and simpler life (if this is even possible given the state of our natural resources) or that pivot will deposit us in the future. Right now, that primitive thing looks more likely.

I think a representative world body with some clout that spent its time brainstorming and collecting ideas, conducting research, and coordinating a space program and even an implementation of that much maligned Agenda 21 are starting to look like a pretty good way to start.

This could be our World War III, a cause larger than any of us that brings us all together.

Hillary Email: The Motherlode
October 31, 2020

Well, there is celebration in Trump-land today but, to me, it all seems just a bit too convenient. All along Republicans have promised to assault Hillary with her rumored crimes all the way to the 2016 election and they have made their promises come true in spectacular fashion. Perhaps they have hit the email motherlode. Perhaps they will finally be able to prove, once and for all, that Hillary is the monster they say she is, and a traitor to boot. Perhaps Hillary will end up in jail.

But I have a lot of questions about the way this all happened. Here we have a "eureka moment" based on evidence that, to my mind, is tainted and a chain of evidence that is, possibly problematic. I certainly do not want to get into any trouble with the FBI. I have no insider information. I am just sitting here speaking from my vantage point in the cheap seats offering a different take on this possibly game changing Friday night email news dump.

First, the fact that a letter was delivered to Congress and news of this hit on a Friday guaranteed that the media would have their proverbial field day speculating about this for an entire weekend. It is also guaranteed that the story would continue to dominate the news cycle because the media stars coming back from their weekend activities would have to weigh in. That timing gave the story major legs, and Trey Gowdy got to be on Joe Scarborough once again when his stunning list of Hillary's stumbles (he means crimes) even made Mika gush about how damning things look.

Second, pardon me for being skeptical, how serendipitous! The dream scenario is delivered unto the Republicans at the last possible moment. But doesn't it seem just a bit too convenient? And isn't Donald Trump just a bit too happy. Finally, he gets the media off his possibly criminal sexual exploits and onto the easier to litigate exploits of Anthony Weiner.

He gets to crow that he was right all along about Huma Abedin and Hillary Clinton. Whenever Trump is crowing, I am miserable.

Third, here we have a laptop of a man who is in the clutches of the courts, who looks like he has been caught in a serious crime, whose wife is leaving him, and who is, therefore, under great duress. This is a man who would make a deal. This is a man who could be talked into anything that might help him stay out of jail. Things could be planted in his laptop, perhaps Wikileaks documents (so they could be leaked from a more acceptable source) or even faked document (although now that there are 650K of these emails phony documents are not so likely). Huma says that she did not have any access to that laptop, but she may have had an email account there, even one opened by her husband. We know that anything can be downloaded into a computer through a thumb drive. I think there are ways that documents could have been placed on that computer after Weiner was arrested.

I have no evidence, just the gut feeling that something is very fishy about this whole new email motherlode twist. All we can do is speculate while we face the increased possibility that we could end up with Donald Trump as the President of the United States of America. Then I am guessing, we will truly see what bad judgment brings when it is practiced on a grand scale.

November

Erasing the Sixties
November 14, 2016

The "military-industrial complex" is finally poised to wipe out the sixties. Almost half of America stayed "straight" while the rest of us grooved to a new beat in the sixties. Change was in the air.

We wanted peace, not war. Our guys were in Vietnam, fighting a war that was not our business, although it was sold as a war against Communism. Since an all-out war on Russia was too risky, we fought them in Vietnam, a tiny nation. It was an awful war, as all wars are, but even more difficult because of the terrain, and the temperatures, and a style of guerilla hit-and-run warfare we were not prepared for. We responded with Agent Orange and napalm and learned that chemical warfare should be considered unacceptable forever after.

America, for once, found a voice of dissent. We wanted out of this war. But we were divided. Some Americans were hawks even in the sixties, who felt that America, when provoked, must respond with military force. There were probably even cynics who believed that war always helped boost the American economy. For some people everything is about money. Many Americans supported the war because they are Americans, they are patriotic, and they had sons, daughters, husbands, fathers in Vietnam fighting this bizarre and deadly war.

We were experiencing a new hostility to the very institution at the foundations of the American economy. It was not hitting home that our democracy was not quite as democratic as we would like nor were our opportunities quite as equal as we would like. Some Americans began to suspect that the powerful people were stacking the deck in their favor and that our money was going to people who were already powerful and rich. The rich and powerful wanted a national government that was in the control of those who believed that we needed a strong military (possibly putting us in line to be permanently at war), and those who felt that if our laws favored industry the American economy would also be the strongest economy in the world. These folks believed that a strong military-industrial complex would keep America dominant on the world stage.

The other half of America railed against the "establishment" and wrote about change, talked about change, and demonstrated for change. This half of America even tried to live in the changed America they hoped was emerging. The straighter half of America grew long sideburns, wore bell bottoms, and went off to work every day. They did not even understand what the "change" chants were all about. They felt that the counterculture was unreal, nonsensical, and possibly treasonous.

These were the days when pressure from people both black and white led to the Civil Rights Act signed in 1965. Passing a law never cures a society's ills like magic. You can make people act in certain ways, but you cannot make them feel certain things. But this law represented the kind of humanitarian changes that resulted from the idealistic and, some believed, airy-fairy view that this was currency in the counterculture. Learning to accept the diverse nature of America's people was very much a part of "hippie" philosophy. In cities we saw more racial mixing than occurred in earlier decades. Concern about poorer Americans become an issue that should not only be addressed by churches, but also by the American government.

And we had the pill, the birth control pill, which gave some women the freedom to control their own futures. They could enjoy physical intimacy without having to accept that this would almost inevitably produce an offspring, either planned or unplanned. Women were already a fixture in the workplace, but now a woman could choose to pursue a serious career, like a man could. Women talked and talked in consciousness-raising groups all over America. It gave women the heady sense that they were not just appendages of men. We were half of humanity, and we were not feeling at all submissive. Why were we given brains that worked so well if we were not intended to share in their culture and contribute to their culture?

There were always establishment forces who hated these movements that began in the sixties. Richard Nixon embodied that snide, entrenched opposition to all things "new age". The side wars between John Lennon and Richard Nixon were perfect representations of how ridiculous and petty his resistance and his fear often seemed. Although John Lennon lived the "revolution" he had too many personal problems to be a real threat. He was essentially an artist, someone who could inspire a counterculture war, but not lead it.

The "establishment" hated the counterculture. Many of the laws, policies, and programs that Republicans hate most have roots in the sixties. The Great Society may not have arisen fully formed in the sixties, but you could see counterculture concerns all over it. The Great Society gave rise to "big government." Even environmentalism tended to split along the lines established in the sixties.

The same decade also gave America a culture split between the Hawks and the Doves. Imperialism, colonialism, American interference in foreign government, regime change were all "old" philosophies of arrogant nations, according to the members of the counterculture. These strategies for control of others were now considered wrong and unsuited to the ideals of a democratic nation. But not everyone. The Republicans did not soften their foreign policy stances. They felt that if America did not remain number one in every arena, then America would no longer exist as a nation. We would give up dreams of empire and become just another less-than-spectacular nation among many.

Conservatives have always been wary of social programs. No social program could be passed without ways to make it onerous built in. People who needed help must be punished for their failure to compete and survive. We do not even know how social programs would have fared if they were offered without blame and without layers and layers of bureaucracy. Can you have both accountability and simplicity or is it something that will always be a paradox.

Many of the people who fell for the things that were broadcast incessantly on Talk Radio and Fox News are the people who never joined the counterculture.

They considered it a passing fancy. They had families to support, and they had to work; hard to do that, but they also had a carrot in front of them. It was the carrot of prosperity, of a legacy for their families, of their own little dynasty that lived and worked nearby, of a retirement of leisure and time to pursue all of the pleasures they had deferred, the carrot of safety and peace. Then the dream began to collapse, one factory at a time, one pension at a time, one housing bubble at a time.

Is the counterculture to blame for their loss? Is this those damn hippies again? No matter. They look to the very same establishment that shafted them to lift them back up. And we all get President Trump. These "straight shooters" think they have elected a new Ronald Reagan. I believe that a President Trump will more closely resemble a Richard Nixon.

Will the sixties really die, or will the movement just go underground training new young people in the use of the "force" so we can clean up the mess when the fever finally burns out? We might have to bide our time for a bit and see what shakes out, but we will stay in touch.

Donald Trump and the Republicans
November 17, 2016

I haven't said much about Donald Trump winning the 2016 election because I don't know what to say.

During his primary rallies, I did discuss what a Trump Presidency might be like. I was really hoping people would not go "there," but when I saw lawn after lawn and truck bumper after truck bumper with Trump/Pence signs and no signs for Hillary Clinton I began to realize that Hillary fans were laying low.

I wrote many articles in favor of Hillary, but unfortunately no one reads my blog. I did not get a lawn sign though, until the last month before the election. I felt intimidated by Donald Trump's casual approach to violence and the way he loved to incite his followers to express their passion for him. I felt very alone with most of my family deciding that Trump would be fine and most of my friends feeling that Bernie got gypped.

I really do not have the slightest idea what Donald Trump will be like as a President. He may be the President of America, but he is not my President. I think he is ruled by adulation. If he feels his audience is slipping away, he will do what he must to win it back. He does behave predictably in that his reactions to all things are personal and emotional, but he is not ideological. He makes a policy statement one day and reverses it the next.

When I read the Elena Ferrante quartet of books about Naples, Italy I was strongly affected by her descriptions of how Fascism remained a factor throughout Italy long after World War II. I guess I thought, beat Mussolini, beat Fascism. But that was not true. There were many tough guys still around who got their way through intimidation, bullying, and baseball bats. That's how I recognized Donald Trump immediately, as soon as he spoke at his first public rally. That's when I began to worry about his ability to sell himself and his willingness to use any means necessary to get his way.

I had studied what the Republicans were up to for the past 6 years. They were the enemy I knew. I didn't like what they were up to. They were planning to pare back the Constitution of 1787, get rid of 200+ years of law and tradition (except the parts that matched their ideology). They have broad plans to benefit the rich and make the poor get off their duffs, but they offer no specifics.

I did not want the Republicans to get control of all three branches of government. They were too radical, they had too many nuts running around shooting off their mouths. They stopped our government until they could win a national election. They cheated and used unfair and perhaps unconstitutional practices to try to make it likely that they would win.

I can't imagine that Donald Trump was part of their plan, but he did win them the coveted office of the President and he won them the right to appoint at least one Conservative to the Supreme Court. And I wouldn't be surprised if pressure was brought to get some Liberals to leave the court. But they may have more than they bargained for in Donald Trump. He has to win and if Congress tries to corner him into doing anything he doesn't want to do or makes him feel that he is not winning, he will find a way to exert his rather frightening authority to get his way. Is he the kind of bully who incites violence but also fears it? Maybe. Another thing we don't know.

My friends and family are smug and thrilled, and they believe that the right person won which is difficult for me to live with. My best course of action is to wait and see what happens. The cast of characters is already making me very nervous, but Donald Trump will not take over completely until after the holidays. Will the Republicans find the strength to resist him if he gets too extreme? Will people rise up in the depths of winter and cry out against things that our democracy should consider unjust? I think the Donald will probably have his way with us. Our best bet is to become what a Facebook group member suggested – Dumbledore's Army. Find a hidden Room of Requirement and train up new Democrats. Hash out great politics and reforms and get ourselves a deep bench. Then, if there is any American democracy left when everyone is done with what Donald and the Republicans have in store for them, perhaps we can try some of the real reforms our government needs.

What the Democratic Party Should Do, Part 2
December 3, 2016

I have been thinking about what the Democratic Party and the Progressives should do next. I include both groups and everyone else on the left because I think we need all hands on deck and because every time I mention the Democratic Party someone schools me on how corrupt and depraved the party is these days with just as many ties to Wall Street and billionaires as are found on the right. Despite all the lectures it will entail I will, henceforth, talk about all of us on the left as the Democratic Party for the sake of brevity. Of course, if we can't really agree that the Party is even a viable and inspirational force these days then perhaps that shows us where we need to begin.

How do we make the Democratic Party a party that people can respect and feel proud to belong to, contribute to, and vote for in elections? Are the days of poverty programs over and should humanitarian benefits that provide for citizens when they are old, or sick, or unemployed become a thing of the past? Perhaps without a robust industrial sector we are not an affluent enough nation to set aside dollars for people who are less fortunate than us? Perhaps we do not pay enough taxes these days to be able to afford programs where our government redistributes our tax dollars back to us in the form of retirement benefits or health care or payments if we become disabled or unemployed.

Programs for People

It has been explained to us that it is today's young workers who pay the benefits of today's seniors, just as our benefits paid for our parents. If there are fewer jobs and if the jobs young people have pay less than people made in the past, then it there still enough to go around? Perhaps Social Security could be redesigned rather than privatized as the Republicans would like. Health care is not paid for in quite the same way, but we have our government deduct extra tax dollars from our pay checks while we are working to pay for most of our health care when we no longer work. Once again costs are apparently exceeding our contribution. These are programs that people like and that offer real benefits to the taxpayers/citizens in our republic/democracy. As a Democrat I have always been proud to think that we support these kinds of benefits for we the people.

And there are many other platforms and policies that Democrats back which still seem important to set a society apart as one that is highly developed, educated, and enlightened. These are the kinds of things that prove a government is absolutely a government of the people, by the people, and for the people. Take away all our social programs and what is left for our government to do – wage war and support business. Our government would then become a government of the wealthy, by the wealthy, and for the wealthy. We are almost there now.

The Party of the Workers

The fact that Americans no longer go off, almost without exception, to work in factories has been a game changer for the Democratic Party. We used to be the party of the working man/woman. Unions and the Democrats were close allies against bosses and wealthy business owners. If workers joined the Democrats their numbers and solidarity gave them clout against the wealthy owner classes. When Republicans tried to take away all government regulation on business and commerce, we the people could dial them back a bit and stave off the worst abuses of unfettered capitalism.

Dems Have Lost Their Worker Mojo

Times have changed in more ways than just where Americans go to work these days. The Democrats have lost their mojo. Workers have had to practically go begging for jobs, and although we have the current push to buck up salaries through passing minimum wage levels that at least cover the essentials required by working families to maintain their homes, afford transportation, and eat and buy clothing, it does not feel the same as when people joined unions and negotiated fairly splendid wages.

The Republicans make a big stink about how the government is getting too big and it is not the business of government to determine the minimum wage for the whole nation, given the differing conditions across the states. But with few factory jobs and with many states passing "right to work" laws which eat away at the power of unions to negotiate for their members, the government is the only entity workers can fall back on now to make sure employers provide a decent wage that meets our current standard of living. Employers have been hit hard by recession and changing markets in America also. They have been known to pay more attention to their bottom line than the needs of their workers. Better to generate plenty of profit and then worry about your employees. Pay yourself first can be carried to extremes without some protections.

Given that the workers no longer require a dedicated party to support labor. Given that there is no longer a matrix of unions for workers to use as a vehicle for negotiating with both employers and government. (Unions still exist but as sort of obsolete institutions, much like medieval guilds, comforting but basically nonfunctional, although public service sector workers still have functioning unions.) Given that retail, which has shown the most growth in offering employment, has never been unionized. Given all these changes it is no wonder the Democrats have lost their footing and are not quite sure how to redefine themselves.

"Identity Politics"

Identity politics is a newly coined type of politics, meaning politics that backs minority groups within our culture that are vocal and that often find themselves up against the reactionary stances of the right in America. Democrats have become the party that backs minorities and defends civil rights of all kinds (even for people who live in America but did not arrive through proper channels). The left strives for equal opportunity and tolerance of diversity, goals which many feel are exclusionary.

White people are already feeling the pinch of so many minority groups which clamor for attention (taking attention away from white folks who, many feel, are the rightful owners of America because the original settlers of America were overwhelmingly white.) Race superiority enters through this door, although some simply never pictured any America other than a white America, and for the latter this becomes a matter of possession as opposed to superiority. People want white tax dollars to go for the needs of white people and not any deadbeat white people either. However, many Americans think that their tax dollars are going to people who just don't want to work, or people who refuse to work for one reason or another. Lots of commenters are saying that the Democrats need to stop using arguments from "identity politics" to sway minority voters to vote left because then we lose those white worker votes that used to make the Democrats so strong. They argue that we need to fight for things that would improve the lives of all Americans and no longer differentiate between groups of Americans.

Democrats, Put Your Money Where Your Mouth Is

I offered my suggestions in my last article, and I asked people to offer their ideas. I got no substantive answers. To repeat my suggestions: use the Democrat organizations that already exist and hold conventions, forums, convocations which make use of speakers but also provide opportunities for attendees to interact. Encourage people who are not already party leaders to speak and get used to speaking in front of groups; train them to develop interviewing skills so they are not shy about talking to the media; get them to sit down and share their viewpoints on important topics for American governance and society and to hash out differences and give the Democrats new ways to talk to Americans that are more progressive, practical, and also aspirational than what we have offered in the past. Spend some money on this. Pay the way for people who cannot afford to attend. Put together some scholarships to send promising people to study politics or law in college. Make an investment in messaging that will work in a post-industrial age and deepen the bench on the left.

Joy Reid's Fifty State Strategy.

This morning I read the article by Joy Reid (don't you just love Joy Reid?) on The Daily Beast website and I found her ideas offered a solution to that huge amount of red we saw on the election maps in 2016. I remember noticing in 2010 or 2011 that Republicans were making a push to control state government and that they had succeeded in 23 states. By 2012 the number of red states was 30. And, as we know, by 2016 it was higher than that. It was the Koch brothers' strategy to spend lots of money on local and state elections and even to use ALEC to send prewritten laws to legislatures which were often passed without revision.

I knew that Republicans were pushing small government and state's rights, and I was not feeling it. I felt it would create a United States that looked more like Europe than America with each state passing its own laws and no uniformity on things like educational standards and job requirements and job safety rules and environmental laws. I also did not like to see wealthy corporate Conservatives playing power games that leapfrogged democratic practices. With Supreme Court decisions like Citizen's United allowing rich donors to spend as many dollars as they wished to influence politics things were looking pretty grim in terms of stopping the momentum of these powerful guys, even if some of the little people saw what they were up to.

Joy Reid suggests that rather than fight these guys we should follow their lead and get right down into the grassroots of politics in each of the fifty states and spend our money to find and elect promising left leaning local people. She feels that state's rights is an area where we might compromise, offering more autonomy to the individual states.

She says, "[but] there's something else Democrats ought to be focused on as they prepare for the long, dark years ahead. It involves trading in a bit of the beloved Hamilton for a dash more of the less morally appealing Thomas Jefferson and embracing what the

Yale scholar Heather Gerken has called "progressive federalism."

There is more to be mined from this article entitled "Best Way to Stop Trump Is At The Local Level" from The Daily Beast, 12.3.2016.

Combination Plan

I see no reason why these two plans offered by two Democrats, albeit one quite a bit more influential than the other, would not work well in tandem. No reason these two ideas couldn't both inform the strategy on the left as we prepare for the next election, a midterm election. We could make a lot of progress in two years, but we must be organized, work together, and begin soon.

This is the Dark Side
December 6, 2016

This is the dark side of the internet. This is where the trolls live and the conspiracy theorists and the authors of fake news. The writing is often dramatic with lots of "documentation" offered and perhaps illusions to organizations of myth and history which we imagine no longer exist, such as the Knights Templar. These folks demonize politicians and people who are rich and famous. They like to create graphic images of them as Satan, suggesting that they worship Lucifer.

Do they believe what they write? Do they think Nancy Pelosi is Lucifer on some days and Hillary Clinton is Lucifer on others? I doubt it but they hope their readers will believe, and some do become converts.

Comments were made on my articles about Hillary which began to refer to things that I did not really understand. They accused her of child abuse, they talked about how "dark" she is, they hinted that she performed criminal acts. These sly comments hinting that Hillary Clinton is some kind of monster began to appear before 2016 voting started, during the early voting and even up to and including election day. I have no idea how much of an effect these conspiratorial whispers had on the election.

Recently the malignant messages came to a head in the attack on a pizza shop in Washington, DC where a guy with a gun entered the establishment with the intention of breaking up a secret pedophilia ring involving Hillary Clinton that was supposedly being run from secret spaces under the pizza shop. Who started this rumor? An article appeared in The Daily Beast on Monday, December 5, 2016, entitled "Pizzagate is the Satanic Panic of our Age But This Time the President's Men Believe It"

After reading this eye-opening article I began to remember the many references to Lucifer that I had been seeing on the Right and the word Illuminati being used as a shortcut to a larger body of thoughts and ideas, but I thought the conspiracy theory ended there. Apparently, this stuff goes way beyond the academic and posits a theory that there is an enormous pedophilia ring and child slavery trafficking operation that has engulfed almost all of our politicians, and in fact, politicians and famous people around the globe.

This activity has been practiced, according to some, by every American President except, Reagan, Carter, and perhaps Nixon. A shadow government has resulted from these nefarious activities which allows financiers and others who know of and have proof of these activities to hold our government leaders (and even EU leaders) under their control, to make them do their bidding for fear of exposure. So, all the while I was saying that Hillary Clinton is hardly nefarious, this conspiracy theory nonsense was enthralling readers on the internet and possibly affecting the outcome of the election. Even the infamous Alex Jones got in on this one, or was, perhaps, the prime mover.

Am I naïve or sane? If this crap these writers are pedaling is in any way true, then our planet is doomed.

I choose not to believe a word of it; it's obviously a conspiracy theory. Who makes this stuff up though? General Flynn's son just got fired for blogging about this bizarre tale, but I don't think he authored the theory; I think he was just repeating what he had read on another site. Why do people make this stuff up? I suppose the answers seem obvious (create fear, get attention, influence events).

Pedophilia and child trafficking are very real though, and it is impossible to ignore the fact that if there is a "product" (in this case a young human being) then there must be a market for that "product". Who are the people who create a market for trafficking such as this? I assume that all our political class is not involved in this. That's the part I believe is fake. But will these particular twisted vices ever be eradicated?

I'm writing about something I find loathsome and that I know very little about, but I am worried because this stuff seems to go way beyond a pizza parlor in Washington DC and therefore it should be on our radar.

We the People – Hypnotized December 11, 2016

Watching DT choose his cabinet is sort of like rubbernecking at a terrible accident. You want to turn away, but you can't. You are hypnotized. All that past-its-prime testosterone on display, my, my. And American women actually thought it might be time to elect a woman as President. Well, our new president elect (not my president) is making it very clear that this is a male, excuse me, white male, dominated world. That makes the spectacle even more fascinating. Watching the kiss-my-ring-courtiers-in-the-anteroom action at Trump Tower made me think I was back in a time dominated by white male kings.

Will this be a cabinet of serpents or of chess players? Probably both types of strategists will be represented in this crew of actors who are distinctly non-political, at least in the sense that we have no knowledge of how they will behave in our American political arena. That is what has us hypnotized. Are we watching the death throes of our American Democracy/Republic? Are we watching a sell-out to Russia? Are we watching savvy businessmen who can put the American economy back on top of the heap? Will there be any rules about what they can or cannot do as they supposedly are somewhat constrained by the American people and the Constitution, or will it be total unfettered Capitalism run amok? Are our American documents resilient enough to make it through to the other side of this onslaught or will we finally be only the Plutocracy we seem to have been headed towards all along?

Yes it is all astonishing, and because we have no idea how this will go, we are somewhat convinced that a wait-and-see attitude might be best. But our brains are screaming that this cannot turn our well. Letting this crew get their hands on American government will turn us into a nation we hardly recognize. Letting these admittedly very successful, but very intolerant and opinionated people control our fate will not bode well for "we the people." After all DT has already told us he does not respect us because we are not successful.

Can we shake ourselves out of our torpor? Can we come out of the tabloid trance induced by our daily news? Perhaps we could start with flash mobs and work our way up to organized demonstrations that will at least register on the Washington Richter Scale. If we come out in large enough numbers, then it might get through to the world that we do not all feel comfortable with our new administration and we wish to be heard. I am as bad as everyone else as I will not be putting together any demonstrations any time soon. It's cold here.

[Side note] At least it feels like the Republicans we used to love to oppose in Congress are also just a bunch of annoying fleas to these "he-men" that surround Trump. (Yes, I know there are women but only in posts that are traditionally considered feminine.) So, although these guys in Congress talk about repealing Obamacare and turning Medicare into a voucher program and privatizing Social Security we have no clue if the new King and his court are even paying any attention in these peons who are so excited to be finally in charge of remaking America in the Conservative image. Does DT have the same agenda as the Republicans? They seem to think so, but I have my doubts.

It is all so engrossing, and yet allowing ourselves to be onlookers is dangerous when our daily lives could be so deeply affected by what our "emperor" decides. Will it be too late once this president-elect becomes the actual president?

I Feel a Great Disturbance in the Force
December 14, 2016

I know that Star Wars is not true. There may be a force that connects us all, but it is not the force that the heroes access in Star Wars. But when that sinister Death Star destroyed an entire innocent planet, it seemed a great metaphor for the terrible destruction we inflict on each other and we wish there was a rebellion we could join without violating our beliefs in a nation's right to autonomy. It is not our fight, but it is our grief. We repeat the words "a great disturbance in the force" because it sometimes expresses exactly how we feel.

(This was a photo essay that included before and after pictures of Aleppo. Refresh your memory with Google images.)

Unfettered Capitalism Wins
December 19, 2016

It is December 19, 2016, the day America's electors decide whether to break with tradition to keep a crazy authoritarian leader from running our nation or not. I am sure that no one is brave enough to keep this man out of office. My mind cannot help but move ahead into the future we are about to usher in. We take a chance on destroying our nation if we accept the electors' votes and install Donald Trump, or if we decide to ignore the electoral college and go with the popular vote and install Hillary Clinton – either way we break with law and tradition.

Even as I await the surely inevitable results an image comes alive in my mind of the conference table at the G8 Summit (yes, we are back to eight nations because I am certain that DT will reinstate Russia). At one end of the conference table will be 'Putie' and at the other end, The Donald, finally face to face and, for the moment, sharing power. Each of these men is determined that fossil fuels and GDP and military might will still determine which nations are most powerful. If we switch away from fossil fuels how will the order of power among nations be determined?

So, the G8 has changed its mission statement and has become the Board of Directors of Planet Earth. It plans to make sure that gas and oil continue to be a currency mill pumping money into the economies of the eight member nations (which could be a different eight nations if membership is determined by fossil fuel production). This old energy, fossil fuel energy will be used to bring back an Industrial Age that has been rapidly morphing into something else, some *je ne sais quoi*. We know that industry is being turned over to robots, with less human fodder required to run the world's engines of manufacturing and commerce, and soon even in service sectors. Perhaps we will turn away from robotics for decades so that the Board can find a use for all the world's extraneous masses.

Because with an exploding world population and less and less work for humans to do what will the leaders do to keep the thumbs of their power on the people, to keep them as useful consumers, but to never allow them to believe that they can have something for nothing. Life should be a "beach" for the wealthy, but for the poor it should be a struggle. We can't have people enjoying themselves all over the place on the public dime. And that will not even be acceptable to poor folks. Most of us expect to have to pay our way in life. But we do not expect the obstacles to be so strong that we cannot get over them or around them with a reasonable amount of effort.

So, given all that, what will this G8 Board of Directors do in this all-Capitalist-all-the time world if we are still earthbound with no technology to expand into space? I don't think it will be pretty for anyone except the top 1%. Human life will be cheap. We will be cheap labor, and no one will mind if our lives become hamster lives – running endlessly on a wheel to nowhere. Perhaps drugs will become plentiful, but I don't think these folks will offer the new peasant class any way out of their servitude.

And when I say that life will be cheap that means that our new Board of Directors will not care if we live or die – in large numbers. Disease may wipe out huge sectors of the population. Violence will also be quite common. Why would the Board require order when they do not have to live anywhere the rest of us live? Building walls will become common – walls to keep us out.

But what will the upper echelons do with their money in such a world. Perhaps they will not go this far just so they still have the world they are used to in which to enjoy their power and success, and people to envy them and wish to join them. Perhaps there will be chances to climb out of the muck and revel in life at the top. Nine billion people is an enormous audience though. Probably too big. Many of us will have to die to keep the population of the planet within comfortable limits. Perhaps the population will always be set to what it was in 1950.

Will there be any concessions to keeping environmental conditions that offer beauty, biological diversity, and fresh air and water? If the Board of Directors is limited to living within the confines of this planet it is safe to say that they will have to find a way to balance their avarice with their survival. It will be interesting to see how they create that equilibrium, if any of us are still around.

A Capitalist dream may take over the minds and hearts of our new global Board of Directors for a while, but even they will soon discover the disadvantages of fouling their own nest. Will they get it in time to save the planet? Maybe not. If does seem as if money makes you stupid.

The Group of Eight (G8) refers to the group of eight highly industrialized nations – France, Germany, Italy, the United Kingdom, Japan, the United States, Canada, and Russia – that hold an annual meeting to foster consensus on global issues like economic growth and crisis management, global security, energy, and terrorism.) *cfi.org*

www.ingramcontent.com/pod-product-compliance
Lightning Source LLC
Chambersburg PA
CBHW032107280326
41933CB00009B/770

* 9 7 8 1 7 3 4 8 6 7 5 1 0 *